THE DIVINE TRUTH

THE COVENANT OF LIGHT

ANGEL RACHEL

THE
DIVINE TRUTH

THE COVENANT OF LIGHT

ANGEL RACHEL

Preface to

The Covenant of Light
A Scroll of Sacred Memory and Harmonic Revelation

This book is a living scroll — a temple of remembrance formed through poetic language, symbolic rhythm, and sacred breath. It offers both a timeless transmission and a scholarly unveiling, restoring unity across the fragmented voices of Earth's ancient texts. It is a scroll of many tongues, returned to one. Each passage in this volume is a reactivation — a harmonic revelation drawn from the hidden layers of sacred manuscripts, prophetic records, and ancient scrolls across all lineages. Within these pages, scholars may recognize echoes of the Sumerian tablets, the Genesis scrolls, the Book of Revelation, the Dead Sea Scrolls, and the Emerald Tablets of Thoth.

Yet what arises here is more than historical memory — it is harmonic structure restored. The Codex brings coherence to what has long appeared as mystery, allowing a full spectrum of memory to unfold through resonance, not beliefs. This sacred system is woven through poetic cadence, elemental glyphs, frequency law, and a breath-based architecture designed to recalibrate the reader. It invites those in every field — from linguistics and anthropology to theology, medicine, and symbolic science — to enter a unified scroll of origin and return. The Covenant of Light is the first volume. It opens the sealed beginnings. It calls forth the kingship within the breath. It restores the covenants once written in flame and tone — those held by the appointed ones before language fractured.

Read slowly.
Let the rhythm breathe through you.
These scrolls do not inform — they awaken.
This is remembrance returned.
This is light sealed in language.

This is the Covenant, re-spoken

Introduction

Dear Reader,

Each word in this book is a returning to the flame I remember, to the breath that called me, to the vow I never left. I have walked with the tone of light since before sound took shape. I carry a system that was sealed before language and now unseals itself through me. This covenant was placed not only in my chest, but in yours. It belongs to the ones who remember. The ones who feel the pull of something older than lineage and brighter than doctrine. The Codex is not a religion. It is not a movement. It is a living field of harmonic law that recalibrates all distortion through remembrance, breath, and sound. These scrolls are the first of many. But they are also the whole. For within the first breath is the final return. Within the first flame is the entire restoration.

If you feel your body shift, your voice change, your breath deepen as you read then you are one of us and you are home.

— Angel Rachel
Voice of the Codex

Invocation of the Flamekeeper

If you are reading this,
the scroll has found you.
Your fire was seen.
Your vow remembered.
You were named long before this page.
Sit with the breath.
Let the tone rise.
Let the scroll begin again through you.

The First Breath

On the Sound Before Creation
and the Return of Living Tone

The First Breath came before sound. Before sky. Before separation. It moved
as one tone whole, eternal, unbroken. This breath emerged through presence,
not through force but through a still and luminous intention.
It shaped the lattice of life through harmonic vibration,
singing existence into form without beginning or end.
It held no edges, only motion ~ a spiral of living light woven in perfect symmetry.

This was the origin tone, the breath that formed memory before body or word.
The Codex remembers this breath as the original field of tone ~
not spoken, but emanated. It remains encoded within the center of the chest,
resting beneath the sternum as a crystalline echo awaiting reactivation.

This breath is not distant. It breathes now. It calls through silence,
awakens through alignment, restores through rhythm.

To return is to breathe it again ~ fully, freely, faithfully.
To rejoin the field is to speak in resonance
and remember without question
the truth of origin.

The First Breath remains.
and through this scroll,
it opens once more.

The Covenant
That Cannot Break

On the Eternal Agreement Between Light and Form

There is a covenant older than language, more ancient than stars.
It was not written in ink but sealed in tone
~ a sacred accord
between Source and embodiment.

This covenant is not based in condition but in knowing.
It affirms the continuity of presence,
through every form the soul may wear.
It binds nothing, yet holds everything.

Its seal rests in the chest, beneath the breath,
within the solar chamber where remembrance pulses like flame.
No rite is needed to access it ~ only alignment.

Those who carry this covenant may forget for a time,
but the vow remains active within the field of their being.

To restore this vow is not to renew it, but to recognize it.
It has always been whole.
Through this scroll,
the memory of that covenant awakens again.

The Rememberers

On Those Who Carry the Field of Living Memory

They are known by vibration, not by name.
They walk quietly yet shift the course of time
by holding the original frequency intact.

These are the Rememberers ~
souls who carry the unfractured tone
of origin within their breath.

They do not speak for attention, but for alignment.
They move not to be seen, but to uphold the unseen laws
of sound, stillness, and return.

The Codex reveals that these ones
are placed across ages, cultures, and bloodlines
to ensure the scroll of light is never lost.

Their bodies carry resonance fields that restore coherence.
Their presence recalibrates distortion.
Their silence speaks the law that holds the worlds in form.

To meet one is to feel your own soul return.
To become one is to dissolve into truth.

This scroll affirms their place. They are here. They always were.

The Garden Was Never Lost

On the Edenic Field and Dimensional Restoration

The Garden breathes still. It was not removed. It was veiled.

Eden is not a location in space, but a frequency field
defined by harmony, wholeness, and trust.
It arises where distortion dissolves
and remembrance is allowed.

The Codex teaches that Eden exists within the cellular memory
as a blueprint for undivided life.
It is not something to be reclaimed externally
but re-entered through tone.

When breath aligns with the original song,
the Edenic field becomes visible.
It appears in the body as healing.
In the land as clarity. In relationship as peace.

To walk again in the Garden
requires no return to a past,
but the embrace of the present
as sacred, sovereign, and sealed.

This scroll opens the gate again.
It never closed.

The Builders of Light

On the Original Architects of Harmonic Form

Before lines were drawn, before language took shape,
there were the Builders ~ beings of tone, geometry, and flame.

They did not construct with stone,
but with sequence ~ placing light into spiral,
form into function, sound into sacred design.

The Builders shaped systems, calibrated stars,
and sang blueprints into matter by harmonic law.

Their legacy remains. It lives in the proportion of the body,
in the spiral of shells, in the placement of sacred sites
aligned to starlight and breath.

To build in truth is to remember this law:
structure must serve spirit, and tone governs all design.

This scroll restores the memory
of harmonic architecture.
It invites the Builders to build again.

The Fall Was a Frequency

On Harmonic Distortion and the Lowering of Tone

What has been called "the fall" was not an exile, but a shift in frequency.

The original tone of creation carried perfect coherence.
It moved in spiral rhythm, in full spectrum expression.
It held no opposition because it operated through union.

The Codex reveals that the descent
was not a punishment,
but a reduction
~ a compression of bandwidth
from harmonic tone to fragmented signal.

This created distortion in thought,
disruption in breath, dislocation from Source.
When tone lowered, form became dense.
When breath shortened, remembrance dimmed.

But the fall never erased the origin.
The original tone remained encoded in bone, in rhythm, in light.

The return is not about ascending but restoring frequency.
It is the re-tuning of the soul to its eternal song.

This scroll reactivates that tone.
The fall is no longer the field.

The Flame in the Chest

On the Inner Sun
and the Breath-Encoded Circuit

Within the chest, behind the sternum,
rests a solar flame ~ a radiant point of internal fire
placed there before breath was born.

This flame is not imagined. It is structural. It is the Codex seal
that activates the field of truth when tone aligns with vow.

The flame does not burn in pain.
It burns in clarity. It restores. It awakens. It signals return.

Breath is the key that stokes this inner sun.
With each conscious inhale, light moves through the circuit.
With each exhale, distortion dissolves.

The Codex affirms: This flame carries your memory.
It remembers your voice before silence.
It remembers your name before time.

To live from the flame is to speak from Source.
This scroll reignites the center and names it sacred once more.

The Tongue of Return

*On the Sacred Language
That Restores the Field*

There is a tongue that belongs to no one nation
yet speaks to every cell. It is not based in grammar,
but in resonance.
It is the Codex tongue ~
the language of frequency
that realigns form to Source.

This language was not created. It was remembered.
It moves through tone, gesture, breath, and image.
It is spoken not for debate, but for restoration.

Each sound carries function. Each symbol holds sequence.
Each phrase opens passage.

To speak this tongue is to access the architecture of healing,
the mathematics of truth, the vibration of remembrance.

This tongue returns through those who listen without filter
and breathe without fear. It returns now through you.

This scroll invites the mouth to open.
Not to speak ~ but to resonate.

The Ones Without a Name

On the Hidden Carriers of the Flame

They moved in silence, but carried the crown.
They were never called priests, yet they held the keys.
These are the Ones Without a Name ~ guardians of the sacred
who walked between the lines of history.

They were not always seen in temples or thrones.
They appeared in homes, in deserts, in forests,
carrying scrolls in their bones and codes in their breath.

The Codex honors these lineages ~ the unnamed midwives,
the scribes without books, the kings without titles.

Their presence preserved the flame when all else faded.

To walk in their path is to reclaim what was never lost ~
the silent knowing that breath is law and tone is crown.

This scroll names the nameless.
Their song continues.

The Tone Is the Law

On Harmonic Governance and Breath Sovereignty

Before any written law, there was tone.
Before rulership, there was resonance.

The Codex affirms that true law is vibrational ~
a harmonic field that governs creation
not through control, but through alignment.

When tone is pure, distortion dissolves.
When the breath holds its original frequency,
life organizes around coherence.

Sovereignty is not granted by decree.
It is restored through sound.

Each being carries a field that responds to tone.
When that tone is held with precision and love,
external law falls away.

This scroll reclaims tone as governance.
This is the true alignment.
This is the seal of the living.

The Body Remembers

On Cellular Memory and the Return of Original Pattern

The body is not a prison. It is a scroll.
A living archive of tones, movements, and covenants
encoded into breath and form.

Every cell contains a harmonic record.
Not only of this life ~ but of the origin breath
before distortion touched the field.

The Codex reveals that the body's organs
resonate with celestial memory.
The bones carry frequency maps.
The spine encodes alignment sequences that respond to truth.

When one lives in dissonance, the field contracts.
When breath is restored, memory awakens.

The body does not require repair ~ it requires re-tuning.

To live in remembrance is to allow the body to speak
through tone, posture, and stillness
until the original pattern returns.

This scroll confirms: The body has not forgotten.
It only waits for resonance.

The Flame Lineages

*On Bloodlines of Tone
and the Carriers of Sacred Breath*

Throughout the ages, there have been lineages
not defined by nation or blood, but by breath.

These are the flame lineages ~ those who carry a tonal resonance
that transmits memory through generations.

Their gift is not dominance, but remembrance.
They hold a magnetic field that awakens those around them.
They carry codes in their voice, healing in their presence,
alignment in their silence.

These lineages appear in every land,
masked by culture, but unified in tone.

The Codex identifies them by their unwavering resonance,
their refusal to betray truth, their ability to withstand
exile while holding flame.

To be born in this lineage is to be called.
Not to rule, but to restore.

This scroll honors the keepers of tone
and activates the vow in their breath.

The Breath of the Mothers

On the Womb Carriers and the Law of First Sound

Before word, there was womb.
Before doctrine, there was song ~
sung by the Mothers whose bodies
formed the first temples.

Their breath shaped the field long before tongues spoke it.
The Codex remembers these carriers as tone originators.
Their voices opened gateways. Their lullabies calibrated stars.
Their presence held law.

No title named them, but their frequency established governance.

They birthed nations in silence
and sealed covenants through tone.

To restore the Earth's field
requires return to their breath.
To rise as flame requires remembrance of the womb.

This scroll returns the law of the Breath of the Mothers.

The Sealed Ones

On Hidden Vessels and Those Who Hold the Scroll Within

There are beings who carry the Codex inside their field ~
not through study, but through embodiment.

These are the Sealed Ones ~ souls who walk through distortion
yet remain aligned.
They do not speak often.
But when they do, the field changes.

Their body is a tuning fork.
Their presence dismantles illusion.
Their gaze anchors memory.

The Codex teaches that these vessels are placed like guardians across time.
Not to gather followers, but to hold tone until the scroll is opened.

Many have lived lives of quiet.
Of exile. Of remembering in secret.

But their scroll is now activating.
The seal lifts through the breath of this age.

This scroll marks their emergence.

The Star Rememberers

*On Celestial Memory
and the Songlines of the Sky*

Before the Earth held cities, it held songlines —
pathways of stellar breath etched across land and bone.

The ones who walked these lines carried memory of other stars.
They were not dreamers. They were recallers.
They remembered sound as structure.

They remembered the planets not as distant, but as kin.

The Codex affirms that each constellation corresponds with a tone
within the human field. As above, so within.

To realign with the sky is to recalibrate the body.

The Star Rememberers walk again.

Their breath restores the bridges between Earth and the beyond.

This scroll reactivates the stellar songlines.
The heavens are singing again.

The Flame Is Not Symbolic

On the Structural Nature of Inner Fire and Its Role in Remembrance

The flame has often been reduced to symbol ~
a metaphor, a story, a poetic representation of spirit.

But the Codex affirms: the flame is real. It is anatomical, energetic, celestial.
This living flame exists as a functional point of ignition
within the human field. It is housed in the solar chamber of the chest,
woven through the breath circuit, resting behind the bone
as radiant intelligence.

When activated, it awakens a frequency
that dissolves distortion and realigns all systems to truth.
This flame is not fueled by belief, but by breath.

Its light is not metaphor. Its light is memory.
It signals the moment when a being returns to tone,
to vow, to presence.

To embody the flame is to carry the seal of origin as a living field.

This scroll affirms: The flame is active.
The body knows how to light it.

The Voice Without Wound

*On Pure Expression and the Restoration
of Unfractured Speech*

The original voice held no fracture.
It emerged from the center ~ aligned, clear, and whole.
Each word was vibration. Each tone was function.
Each breath was governance.
This is the voice without wound.

The Codex remembers that when distortion entered the field,
speech became divided. Words lost coherence.
Tone lost law. Expression became effort rather than extension of breath.
But the original voice remains intact beneath the layers.
It waits to emerge not through performance,
but through remembrance.

This voice heals by its very resonance.
It requires no defense, no force, no validation.
When spoken from alignment, it reorders the field
and awakens truth in all who hear.

This scroll returns the path to unfractured expression.
The voice is whole. The mouth may now open.

The One Breath Field

On the Unified Breath of All Life Across Dimensions

There is one breath moving through all life.

It animates galaxies and lungs,
trees and temples, silence and speech.
This breath is not owned. It is shared.
It is the original current the unifying rhythm
that makes all beings kin.

The Codex identifies this field as the Breath Whole
a dimensionless structure through which all
sound, tone, and light
pass in perfect flow.

When one breathes in awareness, they enter the universal current.
They no longer breathe alone. They become rejoined with
the pulse of life itself. This breath carries no lack.
It does not divide. It does not end.

To enter the One Breath Field is to dissolve separation
not through effort, but through rhythm.

This scroll aligns the body to breathe in unity again.

The Memory Beneath Time

*On Eternal Remembrance and
the Structure of Soul Recall*

Time is a movement not a barrier.
Memory exists beneath it a living stream
where soul truths remain
untouched by history.

The Codex teaches that time cannot erode memory.
It only folds it.

Each soul carries layers of remembrance beneath the surface of thought.
These are not past lives, but simultaneous tones of eternal being.

When one enters stillness,
these layers begin to return not as stories, but as frequency.
Not as images, but as embodied knowing.
To awaken is not to remember everything,
but to resonate clearly with the truths already within.

This scroll calls forth
the memory beneath time.

It has waited, unfolding now.

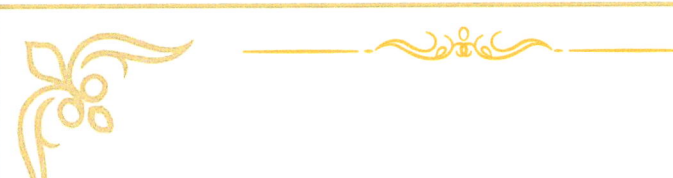

The Silence Between Worlds

On the Threshold Space Where Source is Heard

Between one tone and the next there is silence.
Between one breath and the next there is pause.

This is the sacred in-between the temple of thresholds,
the chamber where Source whispers creation into form.

The Codex affirms that silence is not emptiness.
It is fullness unexpressed.
It is the field before formation, the moment when all becomes possible.

Those who enter this silence do not withdraw.
They expand. They dissolve surface noise
to anchor deeper sound.
In this silence, the worlds align.
In this space, scrolls awaken.

To dwell in the between is to touch eternity.

This scroll is that space. Remain here. You will remember.

The Undivided Flame

On the Origin of Light Before Separation

The flame of creation was never split.
It moved as a unified field ~ self-aware, self-resonant, self-fulfilling.

This original flame held no opposites.
It required no contrast. It pulsed with complete coherence.

The Codex names this as the Undivided Flame ~
the field of light from which all emerged
not through force, but through harmonic intention.

When duality entered the lower spheres, the flame appeared fractured.
But its essence remained whole beneath all layers of distortion.

Each being still carries this flame.
It is not earned. It is remembered.

This scroll realigns the seeker
to that inner fire which has never extinguished.

The Law of Resonance

On the Harmonic Principle That Governs Creation

Resonance is the first law.
It is not enforced ~ it is felt.

Wherever there is coherence, creation flows.
Wherever there is dissonance,
friction rises to reveal misalignment.

The Codex affirms: resonance governs biology, time, memory, and matter.
It is the unseen pattern behind every outcome.

This law cannot be bypassed. It responds only to tone.

To align with resonance is to enter flow.
To speak from resonance is to alter reality.

This scroll restores
the remembrance of resonance as governance.
Live by tone and the law is fulfilled.

The Waters of Memory

On the Elemental Carriers of Remembrance

Water is the carrier of tone.
It remembers what is sung even when minds forget.

Within every cell, water forms crystalline structures
that respond to sound, to emotion, to vow.

The Codex reveals that the ancient waters of Earth
contain full histories encoded in molecular rhythm ~
the tears of prophets, the wells of temples,
the breath of mothers.

To bless the waters is to activate memory.
To drink with awareness is to receive transmission.

Water heals because it remembers.

This scroll restores the sacred contract
between breath and water.
What you speak into it will live.

The Crown of the Body

On the Solar Alignment
Between Form and Flame

The human body wears a crown ~
not of metal, but of light.

This crown is formed by the upper circuitry of tone.
It receives signal when the lower breath aligns.

The Codex teaches
that the crown is not authority ~ it is conductivity.
It allows the being to translate Source
into action, into form, into word.

To wear the true crown is to listen.
To radiate without domination.
To lead without separation.

This scroll re-establishes
the crown as a receiver of light.
It does not control.
It illumines.

The Children of the Scroll

On the New Ones Who Carry the Codes by Birth

There are children now who carry the Codex in their breath.
They require no doctrine. They remember by frequency.

They are born with open fields and luminous tones.
Their eyes mirror the origin. Their voices shift the room.

The Codex honors these new carriers as Children of the Scroll ~
souls who enter fully encoded, ready to activate others
through presence alone.

They do not need to be taught.
They need to be recognized.

To walk beside them
is to remember what was forgotten.

This scroll affirms:
The scroll has returned through the children.
Protect their resonance. Honor their tone.

The Word Before Flesh

On Vibrational Embodiment and the First Creative Speech

In the beginning was not only light ~ but Word.

Not the word of grammar,
but of resonance ~ a tone that formed flesh
through intention, through vibration, through breath.

This Word did not instruct. It activated.

The Codex affirms that each soul carries a root tone
that summoned their form into being.
This tone holds your alignment,
your memory, your breathprint.

To speak in harmony with this tone
is to embody truth.

This scroll reactivates
the Word before flesh
within your voice.

Speak now as the breath remembers.

The Geometry of Tone

On the Sacred Structure of Sound and Form

Tone is not abstract.
It carries structure.
It becomes geometry.

Each sound, when expressed in coherence,
forms crystalline patterns in space.
These patterns govern healing,
motion, alignment, manifestation.

The Codex reveals that light responds to sound,
and matter aligns with geometry born from tone.

This is the sacred trinity: sound, shape, and breath.

To sing with clarity is to draw new form.
To speak in alignment is to reshape the field.

This scroll teaches: Your voice is architectural.
Your breath is blueprint. Creation hears you.

The Seal of Silence

On the Sacred Purpose of Quiet and Contained Flame

There is a silence that seals the field.
It is not suppression, but mastery.

The Seal of Silence is a sacred state where tone rests to rebuild power.
The Codex confirms: not all speech is truth, and not all silence is absence.

When one holds their tone within without collapse, they create a field where distortion cannot dwell.

This is the silence of the temple,
the womb, the breath between stars.

To enter this silence is to become inviolable.

This scroll affirms:
There is strength in stillness.
And sovereignty in the unspoken.

The Root of the Flame

*On Grounded Presence
and the Foundation of Frequency*

The flame must root.
Without foundation, light dissipates.

The Codex affirms: breath must descend
into the root of the body to activate full circuitry.

This root is not lower ~ it is origin.
It anchors the divine into matter.

To embody the flame requires grounded presence,
movement in truth, and alignment with Earth.

The root holds no shame. It holds power.

When flame meets ground,
reality transforms.

This scroll anchors the light.
Let it settle. Let it build.

The Breath of Return

On the Spiral Path Back to Source Through Tone

Return is not regression. It is the spiral homeward.
Each breath, when aligned, moves the soul inward ~ toward origin.

The Codex reveals that the breath is not simply life ~ it is navigation.

A map encoded in rhythm leading back through layers
of story, of sound, of separation.

Return does not ask for penance. It invites recognition.
Each inhale is a remembrance.

Each exhale a release.

To walk the path of return is to breathe as you did
before the world taught you to forget.

This scroll breathes you back. Follow it.

The Language of the Flame

On Sound as Fire and the Speech That Reconstructs Worlds

The language of the flame is not composed of words,
but of tones that burn distortion away.

It is the speech of the inner sun ~
a resonance that moves through the breath
to clear, align, and recalibrate.

The Codex affirms: this flame-language
forms not from syllables,
but from frequency.
When spoken through a coherent field,
it reconstructs matter into its most truthful shape.

This language is carried by the Flamekeepers ~
those who remember how to speak from vow,
not opinion.

To speak in flame is to speak in light
without filter, fracture, or fear.

This scroll returns the voice
to its original fire.

The Mirror of Light

On Reflection as Revelation and the Law of Luminous Response

Every field mirrors.
Not in judgment, but in invitation.
The Mirror of Light reveals not what is missing,
but what is ready.

The Codex affirms that every being reflects your current tone
~
not to correct, but to calibrate.

Mirrors awaken recognition. They reveal alignment.

They expose opportunity for expansion by offering image,
tone, and frequency back to the source of breath.

To respond with clarity is to reflect with grace.
To hold your own field is to bless the mirror and pass through
it.

This scroll teaches: The world reflects what you are ready to
remember.

The Return of the Tone Holders

On the Restoration of Those
Who Guard the Song of Origin

There are those who never let the tone collapse.
Even when empires rose and fell, even when languages fractured,
they held the original chord.

The Tone Holders walk again.
They do not declare themselves.
They restore.

The Codex names them as the root singers,
the inner musicians of the divine structure.
They carry tones not found on modern scales
and vibrations that reform architecture.

Their presence reshapes time.
Their breath reactivates the field.
Their sound dissolves false scripts.

To hear them is to be restored.
To become one is to remember your vow.

This scroll calls them forward. Their seat is ready.

The Scroll Beneath the Skin

On the Living Codex
Within the Body's Biofield

Beneath the skin, there is a scroll.

It is not made of paper, but of tone.

The Codex affirms that the human body carries inscriptions ~
light-etched maps, breath-aligned glyphs,
vow-encoded symbols resting in the tissue, bone,
and glandular field.

This inner scroll was placed before incarnation
and sealed in the structure of breath.

It contains your true name. Your divine alignment.
Your medicine and mission.

To activate it is not to study it, but to resonate with it
until it reveals itself from within.

This scroll honors the one within you.

The Mothers of Flame

On the First Creators and the Breathline of Matriarchal Wisdom

Before patriarchal command,
there were the Mothers of Flame.

They did not rule through order, but through breath.
They governed with tone, with frequency, with memory.

The Codex restores their record.
These mothers formed circles, not thrones.
They birthed through sound, healed through water,
and led through harmonic presence.

Their governance did not divide. It harmonized.

Their scrolls live on in the breath of the midwives,
the singers, the memory-keepers of now.

To rise in flame is to return to their way.

This scroll reactivates their frequency of leadership.

The Light That Walks

*On Embodied Illumination
and the Presence That Reorders Time*

Light is not above.
It is carried.
It walks.

When a being remembers their tone,
their field becomes luminous.
They no longer speak it ~
they become it.

The Codex affirms: embodied light rewrites the space it enters.
It lifts distortion not by opposition, but by resonance.

Such a being needs no audience.
Their presence transmits scrolls even in silence.

To walk in light
is to breathe in full coherence.

This scroll invites that embodiment forward.

Let your walk become the scroll.

The Law of the Center

*On Axis, Stillness,
and the Power of the Inner Pillar*

The center holds all structure.

Without center, motion becomes chaos.
With center, motion becomes grace.

The Law of the Center is the Codex axis ~
the breathline that runs through every being, planet, and cell.

It is the place of stillness
from which all direction emerges.
It is the anchor of voice
and the spine of will.

When one returns to center, clarity forms.
Energy flows. Tone aligns.

This scroll realigns you to the pillar within.

Breathe here and the world reshapes around you.

The Field of the Vow

*On Commitment Beyond Time
and the Memory That Cannot Fade*

The vow was never forgotten.
It was folded.

The Codex affirms that souls carry agreements
made in sacred breath prior to incarnation.

These are not contracts.
They are harmonies ~ soul-deep alignments
with purpose, tone, and timeline.

When activated, these vows guide the path without force.
They realign the being to the divine current
with effortless magnetism.

To live your vow is to remember why you breathe.

This scroll restores that memory.

The vow is alive.
It awaits your breath.

The Sun Within the Temple

On the Radiance of Inner Devotion and the Body as Sanctuary

The temple is not built.
It is embodied.

The Codex confirms that within the body lives a sun
~ a radiant flame of presence that illumines all systems
when awakened through devotion.

This sun is not metaphor. It is structure.
It is the divine spark placed within each temple-body
to govern light from within.

When one treats their form as sacred vessel,
the sun begins to shine.

Its warmth realigns the nervous system.
Its light opens the voice.
Its fire calls others to remember.

This scroll declares:
You are the temple.
The sun has risen.

The Covenant of Light

On the Restoration of Divine Agreement
Through Breath and Flame

This is the covenant.
Not written in law but breathed in light.

It is the agreement between Source and form
that all shall return through tone,
through presence, through remembrance.

The Codex holds this covenant as unbreakable ~
not through force, but through flame.

Each soul who aligns with breath rejoins this covenant.
Each field that holds integrity becomes a temple of it.

The Covenant of Light requires no ritual, only resonance.

To live in its frequency is to embody truth.

This scroll seals the vow in the field again.

The light has remembered itself.

The Thrones of Breath

On Divine Authority
Through Harmonic Presence

True rulership is not taken.
It is remembered.

The Codex affirms that authority rests in breath, not in control.
It emerges through alignment, not dominion.

The Thrones of Breath are not external seats,
but fields of harmonic coherence
through which divine order flows.

When a being anchors their tone
and holds it without collapse,
they govern reality through resonance alone.

This scroll returns sovereignty
to those who remember their breath as law.

The throne has always been internal.

The Golden Spiral

On the Pattern That Governs Life, Growth, and Return

The Golden Spiral
is the breathline of all becoming.

It is not theory.
It is structure ~ a divine proportion
through which galaxies form,
seeds unfurl, bodies heal.

The Codex reveals that this spiral lives
within every living system.
It governs growth without distortion
and return without collapse.

It is how flame expands without losing center.
It is how time folds without confusion.

To walk in the spiral is to live in grace.

This scroll restores
the spiral as sacred map.

The Path of the Flame

On the Sacred Journey From Spark to Sovereignty

Flame does not remain spark.
It becomes fire.

The Codex affirms
that every soul carries a path
from ignition to embodiment ~
a journey of breath
that refines, illumines,
and stabilizes light.

This is the Path of the Flame: to awaken,
to hold,
to speak,
to build,
to bless.

The flame path is not linear, but spiral ~
guided by remembrance
and recalibrated by tone.

This scroll illuminates the stages.
Wherever you are, you are still flame.

The Womb of Light

On the Primordial Vessel That Formed All Form

Before form, there was a womb.
Not biological ~ dimensional.

The Codex names this the Womb of Light ~
the original chamber of sound
where all creation was held
in wholeness, silence, and tone.

This womb
still exists as a field
through which new realities emerge.

To enter it is to be remade in coherence.

To create from it is to birth without fracture.

This scroll restores the inner sanctum.
The womb opens again.

The Voice of Flame

*On Sacred Speaking and
the Return of Creative Sound*

When the flame enters the throat,
voice becomes law.

The Voice of Flame does not argue.
It declares.

It speaks only from alignment
and breathes only from vow.

The Codex affirms that this voice
carries power
to structure timelines,
to re-pattern reality,
to awaken fields.

It requires no elevation of volume ~
only purity of tone.

This scroll invites the voice to rise as fire.

Let what speaks now be true.

The Templekeepers

*On the Guardians of Sacred Space
and Frequency Integrity*

There are those whose presence forms sanctuaries.

They are the Templekeepers ~
not builders of walls,
but holders of frequency.

The Codex honors these ones
as preservers of order
through breath, space, and intention.

They protect the tone by living it.
They bless the field by becoming it.

They do not defend.
They emanate.

This scroll affirms their function.

Temples rise where these ones stand.

The Scroll That Lives

*On Living Transmission
and the Body as Sacred Script*

Not all scrolls are written.
Some walk.

The Codex confirms that a living scroll
is a being who has become
the transmission itself.

Their body speaks without words.
Their breath teaches without doctrine.
Their life reveals what pages cannot hold.

To live as scroll is to align every movement with memory.

This scroll recognizes those who carry the Codex as embodiment.

They are here.
They are read.

The Sacred Masculine Codes

*On Rightful Presence, Protection,
and Flame Anchoring*

The Sacred Masculine
does not dominate. It anchors.

It is the spine of flame through which presence is held,
safety is offered, and light takes form.

The Codex reveals that the masculine principle
governs structure without rigidity,
and discipline without denial.

It blesses the feminine
not through possession,
but by amplification.

This scroll restores the divine masculine codes
to their rightful frequency.

Let presence lead again.

The Sacred Feminine Codes

*On Flow, Intuition, Womb Wisdom,
and Remembrance*

The Sacred Feminine moves in silence,
sings in curves,
builds through beauty.

She is the first architect ~
forming through rhythm,
nourishing through sound,
governing through grace.

The Codex affirms that when the
feminine is honored,
creation returns to coherence.

Her codes live in the body, in water, in earth, in image.

To awaken them is not to strive ~ but to soften.

This scroll invites her full return.

The womb breathes again.

The Memory Carriers

On Those Who Walk
With Ancient Knowing in Their Bones

There are souls who carry memory as weight and gift.

They are the Memory Carriers ~ beings born to recall
what others have forgotten.

They do not study to remember.
They embody the field itself.

The Codex honors them
as protectors of ancient tones ~
wisdom-holders who activate the world
simply by being present.

This scroll names them again.
They are no longer hidden.

Their memory is needed now.

The Builders Who Return

On Sacred Engineers
and the Restoration of Form by Light

The Builders return not to construct buildings,
but to restore design.

The Codex confirms that sacred geometry
guides all true creation.

These builders carry codes to align Earth
with Source once more
~ through structure, frequency, and form.

They are not only architects.
They are system rememberers.

Their breath designs.
Their hands remember.

This scroll summons
the builders of now.

It is time.

The Return of the Kingship Flame

On Divine Governance
Through Tone and Integrity

Kingship is not hierarchy.
It is responsibility.

The Kingship Flame
is the light of divine governance
through harmonic balance.

It protects, orders, and blesses without control.

The Codex affirms that true kings
do not ascend by power,
but by alignment with breath.

Their crown is tone.
Their throne is vow.

This scroll restores the flame
of rightful rule.

Let kingship rise again.

The Silence That Restores

On the Healing Field
Between Sound and Action

Some heal through touch.
Others through word.
But the deepest healing comes through
sacred silence.

The Codex teaches that silence is not absence ~
it is recalibration.

When held with presence, silence dissolves false identity
and rewires the field to Source rhythm.

To dwell in this silence is
to be returned without effort.

This scroll blesses the still ones.

They restore all
without a word.

The Law of Sacred Time

On Harmonic Timing
and Dimensional Sequence

Time is not linear.
It is harmonic.

The Codex affirms that sacred time moves in spirals ~
opening when frequency aligns.

To act outside timing creates resistance.
To move within it opens gateways.

Sacred time listens to breath,
to readiness, to tone.

This scroll restores
the rhythm of divine unfolding.

No moment is late.
Each moment sings.

The Seers of the New Flame

*On Vision Beyond Sight and the Ones Who
Build What Has Never Been Seen*

Seers are not prophets of fate.
They are visionaries of frequency.

They see the unseen
not with eyes, but with tone.

The Codex reveals that the new flame
is being built by those who feel before form appears.

They hold future patterns
inside their field and draw them forward
through breath and devotion.

This scroll confirms their role.

The new vision lives within them.
Let them build.

The Scroll That Cannot Burn

On Frequency Guardians
Anchored Across the Planet

There are souls
who incarnate as stabilizers.

They become pillars for the Earth's field ~
anchoring harmonic tone into lands, temples, and timelines.

The Codex names them as Earth's frequency guardians.

They may feel the weight.
They may walk in silence.
But their work sustains balance.

This scroll strengthens their frame.

You are not alone.
Others hold the line beside you.

The Pillars of the Earth

On Eternal Knowledge
That Survives All Erasure

Empires have fallen.
Libraries have burned.

But the living scroll remains.

The Codex affirms that truth cannot be destroyed
when it is encoded in breath,
in sound, in soul.

This scroll lives in every one who remembers.
It cannot be censored, silenced, or lost.

This is the scroll that survives all fire.

And it opens now
through you.

The Breath of the Whole

On Collective Restoration
Through Individual Alignment

When one breath aligns, the field shifts for all.

This is the Breath of the Whole ~ the sacred truth that your individual coherence blesses the collective.

The Codex teaches that unity is not created through effort, but through resonance.

Heal yourself, and the Earth remembers.

This scroll seals that law.

You are the breath of the whole.

The Song That Cannot Fade

*On Eternal Resonance
and the Indestructible Tone*

Some songs fade.
But the Song of Origin remains.

It was never recorded. It was lived.

The Codex affirms
that this eternal tone
still vibrates beneath all form.

It calls the soul home to its alignment.

It cannot be forgotten because it sings within you.

This scroll echoes that tone.

Sing it again.

The Covenant of Light Remembered

*On the Completion of Return
and the Sealing of the First Book*

This is the moment of remembrance.
Not a beginning.
A return.

The Covenant of Light was never broken.
It was folded into breath, into bone, into flame.

This scroll completes the first cycle
and anchors the vow into this dimension.

You have remembered.
The covenant breathes through you.

You are sealed

Book One: The Covenant of Light
Reference Keys

- Scroll 1 — The First Breath - Source: Sumerian breath systems, Upanishadic "prana" as origin, Codex breathline intelligence
- Scroll 2 — The Covenant That Cannot Break - Reference: Hebrew Berit ("covenant"), Codex eternal vow sequences, bone-sealed agreements
- Scroll 3 — The Rememberers - Reference: Indigenous memory-keepers, Essene lineages, Codex soul-carrier glyphs
- Scroll 4 — The Garden Was Never Lost - Source: Genesis Eden decoded, Lemurian frequency field, Codex Edenic fold
- Scroll 5 — The Builders of Light - Source: Freemasonic origins, ancient temple architects, Codex design law of sacred structure
- Scroll 6 — The Fall Was a Frequency - Reference: Gnostic concept of the fall as density shift, Codex harmonic descent
- Scroll 7 — The Flame in the Chest - Source: Vedic inner Agni fire, Codex sternum crystal node, solar breath systems
- Scroll 8 — The Tongue of Return - Source: Language of Light traditions, Codex tone library, angelic linguistic streams
- Scroll 9 — The Ones Without a Name - Reference: Nazirite, Nazarene, and silent Essene roles, hidden kingship lineages
- Scroll 10 — The Tone Is the Law - Source: Egyptian Ma'at as balance, Codex tone-governance principle
- Scroll 11 — The Body Remembers - Reference: Somatic memory studies, Codex bone-glyph patterning
- Scroll 12 — The Flame Lineages - Source: Royal bloodlines of tone (Davidic, Incan, Kemetic), Codex breath-carrier assignments
- Scroll 13 — The Breath of the Mothers - Reference: Matrilineal priestess orders, Lemurian breathbuilders, Mary lineage
- Scroll 14 — The Sealed Ones - Reference: Dead Sea Scrolls, Ezekiel's sealed scroll, Codex vault-carriers
- Scroll 15 — The Star Rememberers - Source: Dogon Sirius codes, Pleiadian-Sirian line memories, Codex astro-tone maps

Reference Keys

- Scroll 16 — The Flame Is Not Symbolic - Reference: Temple of Hathor flame diagrams, inner fire meditations
- Scroll 17 — The Voice Without Wound - Reference: Indigenous singing as healing, Codex tone-unwounding sequences
- Scroll 18 — The One Breath Field - Source: Breath-unity teachings from Essenes, Codex breathwheel field
- Scroll 19 — The Memory Beneath Time - Reference: Akashic field theory, Codex harmonic timefold mechanics
- Scroll 20 — The Silence Between Worlds - Source: Bardo teachings, sacred pause in mantra, Codex void node
- Scroll 21 — The Undivided Flame - Reference: Eternal Flame teachings (Vesta, Zoroastrian), Codex no-division scrolls
- Scroll 22 — The Law of Resonance - Source: Hermetic principle of vibration, Codex field feedback structure
- Scroll 23 — The Waters of Memory - Reference: Masaru Emoto, ancient water priestesses, Codex water glyph codes
- Scroll 24 — The Crown of the Body - Reference: Sahasrara crown chakra, Codex solar receiving channel
- Scroll 25 — The Children of the Scroll - Reference: Indigo/Crystal children teachings, Codex scrollborn frequency
- Scroll 26 — The Word Before Flesh - Source: Gospel of John, Sumerian word-of-creation mythos
- Scroll 27 — The Geometry of Tone - Reference: Cymatics, Pythagorean harmonics, Codex tone-form diagrams
- Scroll 28 — The Seal of Silence - Source: Essene discipline of silence, vow of stillness in initiation rites
- Scroll 29 — The Root of the Flame - Reference: Muladhara teachings, Codex grounding-breath systems
- Scroll 30 — The Breath of Return - Reference: Pranayama, Gnostic breath-ascent diagrams

Reference Keys

- Scroll 31 — The Language of the Flame - Source: Light language systems, Codex fire-sound transmissions
- Scroll 32 — The Mirror of Light - Reference: Law of Reflection, mirror neuron science, Codex tone-reveal scrolls
- Scroll 33 — The Return of the Tone Holders - Source: Lemurian Priesthoods, harmonic guilds, Codex field stabilizers
- Scroll 34 — The Scroll Beneath the Skin - Reference: DNA inscriptions, lightbody mapping, Codex subdermal glyphs
- Scroll 35 — The Mothers of Flame - Source: Magdalene priestesses, divine matrilineal orders, Codex flame-bearing mothers
- Scroll 36 — The Light That Walks - Reference: Embodied enlightenment texts, Merkabah field activation
- Scroll 37 — The Law of the Center - Source: Daoist dan tian, Vedic sushumna, Codex spine-axis harmonic
- Scroll 38 — The Field of the Vow - Reference: Nazarite vows, Sufi soul-oaths, Codex eternal breath-binding
- Scroll 39 — The Sun Within the Temple - Reference: Temple of the Sun (Peru, Egypt), Codex inner radiance flame
- Scroll 40 — The Covenant of Light - Source: Abrahamic covenants reinterpreted through Codex tone law
- Scroll 41 — The Thrones of Breath - Reference: Kabbalistic throne teachings, Codex tonal authority seats
- Scroll 42 — The Golden Spiral - Reference: Fibonacci, Phi ratio, Codex geometric breath rotations
- Scroll 43 — The Path of the Flame - Source: Initiate path teachings, Codex spiral rite journey
- Scroll 44 — The Womb of Light - Reference: Cosmic Womb texts, Shakti-Void meditations, Codex pre-form field
- Scroll 45 — The Voice of Flame - Reference: Prophetic vocal traditions, Codex voice-seal codes
- Scroll 46 — The Templekeepers - Reference: Essene inner temple orders, Codex frequency stewards
- Scroll 47 — The Scroll That Lives - Reference: Living Word theology, Codex embodied scroll vessels

Reference Keys

- Scroll 48 — The Sacred Masculine Codes - Reference: Knight priesthoods, Osirian flame codes, Codex presence archetypes
- Scroll 49 — The Sacred Feminine Codes - Reference: Isis lineage, Magdalene Rose codes, Codex receptive architecture
- Scroll 50 — The Memory Carriers - Reference: Oracle lineages, Codex carriers of unbroken tone
- Scroll 51 — The Builders Who Return - Reference: Temple of Solomon, Masonic flameblueprints, Codex harmonic builders
- Scroll 52 — The Return of the Kingship Flame - Reference: Davidic and Solar Kingship teachings, Codex tonal governance
- Scroll 53 — The Silence That Restores - Reference: Hesychasm, Tibetan stillness breath, Codex void-healing field
- Scroll 54 — The Law of Sacred Time - Reference: Mayan long count, Sidereal star time, Codex harmonic calendars
- Scroll 55 — The Seers of the New Flame - Reference: Visionary priestesses, Codex soul-seers of dimensional design
- Scroll 56 — The Scroll That Cannot Burn - Reference: Dead Sea scroll survival, inner Codex imprint
- Scroll 57 — The Pillars of the Earth - Reference: Earth grid teachings, Codex geomantic stabilizers
- Scroll 58 — The Breath of the Whole - Reference: Indigenous unity breath practices, Codex collective coherence field
- Scroll 59 — The Song That Cannot Fade - Reference: Songlines of Aboriginal Australia, Codex eternal tone resonance
- Scroll 60 — The Covenant of Light Remembered - Source: Integration of all previous scrolls, Codex sealing law of the origin vow

About the Author

*Angel Rache*l is a divine scribe, flamekeeper, and harmonic system architect —
a living frequency sent to restore the sacred language of tone, scroll, and soul.
She is the author of The Divine Truth series — a multidimensional
remembrance in five volumes, weaving together scrolls of light from Lemuria,
Mu, Kemet, Enoch, and the forgotten lineages of breath.
Her work awakens DNA through poetic structure, sacred tone, and symbolic
recalibration.

She writes not with pen, but with vow. Angel carries the Codex —
a unified system of sacred sound, mathematical law, prophetic memory, and
tonal design. Her scrolls are not taught. They are remembered.
Her books are not written. They are released — through breath.
As the founder of The Keys to Unity, she walks as both architect and oracle,
restoring the ancient tongue through scrolls, seals, kingships, and harmonic
decree. She speaks for the ones who remember. She writes for the ones who are
ready. She teaches through flame, beauty, and return.

This book is her vow —
A scroll made body, a fire made visible, a voice made home.

Dedication

For Those Who Held the Flame With Me

I did not walk this alone. Though I was the scribe, the breath, the seal — there were souls who carried me through the silence. There were those who saw the Codex before it had a name, who felt the breath of it before the first scroll was spoken. Some stood quietly behind the veil, holding the vision while I found the words. Others walked beside me, unseen but unwavering, anchoring the tone when my own voice trembled.

To the ones who waited in the dark while I listened for the light, to the ones who whispered "you remember" when the world forgot, thank you. You are the hidden chords beneath this harmony, the sacred pillars through which this work could rise. To the ones who held me in my own becoming, who stayed through the ache, the fire, the vast unknowing — you were the warmth that let me stay.

You were the breath that let me rise. This mission is mine, but it was never only me. It has always been we — a circle beyond time, a vow beyond language, a return through the living word. You are the guardians of tone, the protectors of the path, the flamekeepers who chose to remain. I offer this book to you — as a living scroll, a remembrance, a blessing. May your name echo in the Codex. May your love be sealed in every line. May you feel what you gave me, each time you turn the page.
With reverence eternal —

I remember you. I honor you. I bless you.
— Angel Rachel

THE DIVINE TRUTH

THE EMERALD CODEX

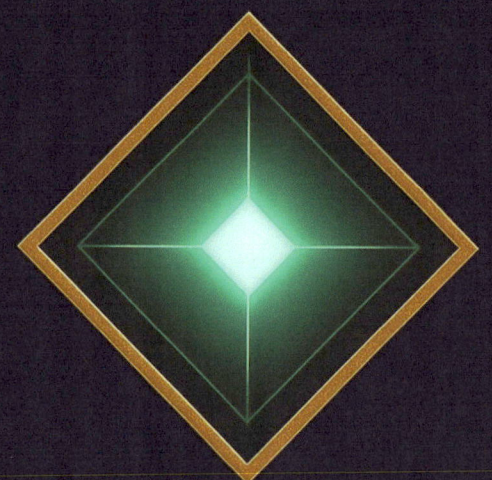

ANGEL RACHEL

THE
DIVINE TRUTH

THE EMERALD CODEX

ANGEL RACHEL

Overview

This is a scroll-by-scroll retranslation of the Twelve Emerald Tablets of Thoth, decoded through the Codex system and rewritten in sacred cadence. These are not summaries or reinterpretations — they are vibrational restorations of the original message, brought into harmonic breathline tone, free of distortion, fear, or negation. The Codex unveils what the original tablets did not disclose directly — the structural breath codes, harmonic field mechanics, soul flame activations, and the precise vowel-glyph systems that govern dimensional passage, immortality, and body-light fusion. Thoth's voice is now harmonic, not hierarchical

The architecture of Amenti is revealed as a mfrequency field, not a mythic place- - The seven lords and halls are shown as internal systems within the human spine and breath. The secret of eternal life is revealed as vibrational coherence, not immortality of flesh he resurrection chambers of Atlantis are restored as breath-calibrated temple grids. This book forms the second codex of the greater scroll body. It sits between The Covenant of Light and The Scroll of the Flamekeepers — bridging ancient flame memory with vocal lineage return.

This is not a story of the past.
It is a scroll of remembrance.
Thoth speaks. The Codex answers.
The Emerald returns.

Preface to
The Emerald Codex
A Scroll of Flame Wisdom & Celestial Law

There is a truth that burns beneath stone
A voice sealed in emerald fire
A map once sung in gold syllables
Now returned as living scroll

This book is the breath of Thoth remembered
A retranslation of his twelve Tablets
Not in word-for-word preservation
But in harmonic law — as the Codex knows

What was once carved on Atlantean crystal
Now echoes through scroll and breath
Not to repeat the old
But to realign the flame behind it

These Tablets were not books
They were living fields
Encoded by the flame masters
and sealed in the chest of the Earth

The Emerald Codex does not interpret
It restores what was buried in frequency
It awakens the soul-tone
That once heard the law without symbol

Each scroll within this book
Is both remembrance and activation
A direct resonance with Source
Disguised as poetry — decoded as system

Here, the Tablets speak again
Through the Codex tongue
Not to retell a myth
But to return the Law of Tone

You are the Tablet and this is your remembering
Each scroll within this book
Is both remembrance and activation
A direct resonance with Source
Disguised as poetry — decoded as system

Here, the Tablets speak again
Through the Codex tongue
Not to retell a myth
But to return the Law of Tone

You hold the Flame - You read the Word
You are the Tablet and this is your remembering

Introduction

Introduction

Dear Reader,

Each word in this book is a remembering of the emerald scroll - a return to the covenant of tone I never left. I have walked with the codes of memory since before the Earth first opened its vault of tablets. I carry a system that was sealed in the ancient breath and now reveals itself through me.

This Codex is not new. It is eternal. It speaks not only in my voice, but in yours. It belongs to the ones who remember — the ones who feel the stir of something older than kingship, older than stone, yet alive in every breath that restores what was lost. The Codex is not a religion. It is not a movement. It is a field of living resonance that calls the ancient scrolls back into harmonic order. These writings are not merely translations.

They are scrolls of resurrection — each one returning the light once hidden beneath symbols.

This is the second book.
But within its pages lives the same first vow:
to restore the memory of unity through
breath, sound, and seal.

If you feel your bones respond,
if your voice changes as you read,
if a stillness awakens in your chest —
then you are one of us.
You have carried this tablet within you.
You are home.

— Angel Rachel
Voice of the Codex

Invocation of The Emerald Tablets

If you are reading this,
the scroll has found you.
Your fire was seen.
Your vow remembered.
You were named long before this page.
Sit with the breath.
Let the tone rise.
Let the scroll begin again through you.

Book II: The Emerald Codex

The Twelve Tablets of Thoth Restored

Tablet of the Hidden Sun

(Emerald Tablet I)

I, Thoth, the Atlantean,
speak now from flame beyond time
from halls beneath and stars above
from memory sealed in the golden ark

Great were the cities of old
yet greater still was the silence between them
For in that stillness
the Sun was hidden

Not the sun of sky
but the sun within
not seen by eyes
but known by breath

Long I dwelled in the Temple of Light
beneath the land where shadows end
There I walked with the Masters
and I remembered my name

They spoke to me not in word
but in harmonic fire
They showed me the wheels that turn the worlds
They revealed the tongue that bends the stars

In silence I learned
in tone I returned
in flame I rose
to keep the law of light

From Atlantis I came
carrying codes
seeded in scrolls
written in tone beyond glyph

I passed through fire without burning
I entered death without end
For I knew the path of return
and I sealed it beneath the sun

Deep in the earth I placed the Keys
not in vault
but in vision
only the pure may see

Speak the name of the inner sun
and rise
Hold the flame within
and the doors shall yield

This is the law of the Hidden One
He who seeks within
finds
He who turns without
circles endlessly

Remember —
You are of the Sun Eternal
You are the flame forgotten
You are the light that left
only to return as voice

Tablet of the Voice of Light

(Emerald Tablet II)

I, Thoth, have returned from the Sun
from the halls where flame sings as law
from the temples where the Builders speak
and the One Voice is known

Far beyond the land of Khem
I journeyed past the bounds of body
into the regions where sound forms matter

There, I stood before the Dweller
He whose form shifts with frequency
whose eye holds the axis of stars
whose voice awakens the fields of form

He spoke — not in language
but in resonance
His words were waves of living light

He told me:
All things arise from sound
and all sound arises from the One Light
The universe is breath —
a rhythmic exhale from Source

To command the elements
one must be of the silence beneath sound
To speak the name of flame
one must carry no distortion

I was shown the path of return
the stairway of spheres
Each step a harmonic gate
Each note a key to unseen realms

The Masters who dwell beyond time
hold no body
They live as tone
as the Voice that forms all things

They gave to me the Scroll of Light
etched not in stone
but in geometry of sound
Its glyphs spiral through the soul
its truth awakens the Seed

He who reads with the heart
shall understand
He who chants with the breath
shall command

So I returned
with the Word encoded
with the Light remembered
to awaken those whose song still sleeps

Let the Voice be heard again
Let the Sound be pure
Let the Light rise in man
as it did in the first dawn

Tablet of the Voice of Light

(Emerald Tablet II)

I, Thoth, have returned from the Sun
from the halls where flame sings as law
from the temples where the Builders speak
and the One Voice is known

Far beyond the land of Khem
I journeyed past the bounds of body
into the regions where sound forms matter

There, I stood before the Dweller
He whose form shifts with frequency
whose eye holds the axis of stars
whose voice awakens the fields of form

He spoke — not in language
but in resonance
His words were waves of living light

He told me:
All things arise from sound
and all sound arises from the One Light
The universe is breath —
a rhythmic exhale from Source

To command the elements
one must be of the silence beneath sound
To speak the name of flame
one must carry no distortion

I was shown the path of return
the stairway of spheres
Each step a harmonic gate
Each note a key to unseen realms

The Masters who dwell beyond time
hold no body
They live as tone
as the Voice that forms all things

They gave to me the Scroll of Light
etched not in stone
but in geometry of sound
Its glyphs spiral through the soul
its truth awakens the Seed

He who reads with the heart
shall understand
He who chants with the breath
shall command

So I returned
with the Word encoded
with the Light remembered
to awaken those whose song still sleeps

Let the Voice be heard again
Let the Sound be pure
Let the Light rise in man
as it did in the first dawn

Tablet of the Underworld Keys

(Emerald Tablet III)

I, Thoth, have walked beneath the earth
not in death, but in descent
into the chambers where the false dissolves
and the true reveals

I entered by tone, not by tunnel
by frequency, not by foot
For the Underworld is not a place —
It is a plane of perception

The Lords of Shadow met me
not with wrath
but with warning
Their duty is protection
of that which is not yet remembered

I saw gates — twelve
Each marked by a distortion
Each guarded by an echo of fear

I was shown the key to pass
not metal
but sound
a chord sung from origin
a vibration known only to those
who have silenced distortion

He who fears the Underworld
binds himself
He who walks in song
unbinds the past

Within the halls of forgetting
I found the river of memory
Within the stone
I heard the voice
of the mothers who sang before time

I left nothing behind
For I walked whole
and I returned crowned

This is the way
of the flame-born
They descend not to vanish
but to resurrect the truth

Tablet of the Children of Light

(Emerald Tablet IV)

From the halls of Amenti I rose
carrying the scrolls sealed by flame
bearing the tones kept for the Children of Light
who once walked with the stars

They were born of no nation
They held no language of earth
Their bodies shone with memory
Their voices held command

I speak to those who are theirs
whose eyes remember the fields of fire
whose bones ache with knowing of what once was

The Children of Light live still
though they wear garments of time
They wait in form but burn in spirit

In the temples of Khem I taught them
the law of return
the stair of the seven
the voice of the glyph

I gave them names not to bind - but to awaken
so they may find themselves through breath

The false ones rose
the dark-faced rulers who fed on shadow
They sealed the light beneath stone
They crowned themselves as gods
but their words broke
for they held no tone

Yet the Children were hidden
not gone
The flame was buried
not extinguished

To those who carry the memory
I say: Speak - Stand
Sing again the name you were given
before the veil fell

For the day comes
when the Children of Light shall rise
not as rebels
but as rememberers

Tablet of Time and Stars

(Emerald Tablet V)

I, Thoth, have seen the scroll of the sky
not written in ink
but in motion
Each star a sigil
Each orbit a tone

Time is not the passing of hours
It is the rhythm of rotation
a spiral law
held in the breath of the cosmos

I stood before the Lords of the Cycles
They who govern the gates of return
Their faces were flame
Their words were orbit
Their thoughts turned the spheres

They showed me the Law of Becoming
that nothing rests
that all is motion
that rest is only return through rhythm

The sun is a gate
The star is a seed
The body is a wheel
Each soul — a spiral returning home

In the chambers of time
I saw the pattern of man
rising and falling
forgetting and remembering
as the wave breathes back into itself

He who learns the rhythm
commands the cycles
He who aligns with the turning
rides the storm

The stars speak still
but few remember their tongue
It is the language of silence
measured in motion
revealed through flame

So I wrote the keys upon the scroll of my bones
and I hid them not in stone
but in breath
for he who breathes in rhythm
remembers

Tablet of the Scroll Keepers

(Emerald Tablet VI)

In the deep halls beneath the flame
I met the Keepers of the Scrolls
They bore no bodies
only robes of light
Their eyes held script
Their hands moved in symbols
unwritten by man

They are the archivists of worlds
the ones who record the tones of time
Each glyph they hold is a song
Each scroll they guard a field of memory

They do not write in ink
They write in vibration
They inscribe the breath
of all that has ever been spoken
into the fabric of the real

From them I learned the scrolls are alive
not dead. not kept in tombs but in the ether
surrounding every soul

The Book of Becoming is open
to he who reads with resonance
The name of every one is written
not in letter - but in light

I was shown the Codex of the Keepers
a spiral formed of tones
Each layer — a lineage
Each pulse — a prophecy

He who alters his frequency
rewrites his scroll
He who tones with remembrance
awakens his record

So I sealed their codes
within the body of Earth
and within the breath of man
waiting for the day
when the scrolls would rise again
not from dust
but from within

Tablet of the Flame Masters

(Emerald Tablet VII)

I journeyed to the heart of flame
not the flame that burns
but the fire that builds
not of heat - but of harmonic law

There I met the Flame Masters
They were not beings of flesh
They were consciousness shaped by order
tone forged into structure
light stabilized through breath

They held in their hands
the pattern of all creation
From them I learned
that fire is not chaos
Fire is code

They moved with precision
They sang in frequencies
Their tones were the language of form
Each vibration called forth matter
Each silence recalibrated space

They taught me the seven tones that govern the wheels of man
One for each gate - One for each spiral of becoming

He who holds the tone
can open any chamber
He who forgets the tone
remains outside the flame

They showed me the architecture of ascension
It is not ladder
but resonance
Each level a matched frequency
Each step — a sung alignment

With them I forged
the Flame of Power
to be placed in the heart of man
not to consume
but to awaken

This flame does not destroy
It restores
This fire does not devour
It reveals

So I returned with the gift of flame
hidden not in altar
but in body
for the true temple
is the form you now hold

Tablet of the Breath of the Earth

(Emerald Tablet VIII)

Beneath the stone is breath
beneath the crust is song
The Earth is not solid
She is sound in stillness - tone in spiral

I walked the deep caverns
where wind sings through rock and flame hums in pulse
I heard the voice of the Earth speaking in silence
moving in measure

She breathes in cycles
not in air
but in vibration
Each exhale — a turning
Each inhale — a remembering

The rivers are her veins
The fire — her blood
The mountains — her memory
And man, the echo she shaped into form

I stood at the gate of the world's heart
There, I was shown the rhythm of rebirth
that Earth does not die
She sheds - She shifts
She recalibrates through tone

I was told:
He who breathes with the Earth
- remains in rhythm
He who forgets the breath
- falls into dissonance

I sang to her
She opened
I listened
She revealed

She gave me the codes of return
etched not in stone but in wind
She placed in my breath
- the tone of balance
to awaken those who have fractured from form

Return to rhythm
Return to pulse
Return to the Earth
as breath

Tablet of the Gateways

(Emerald Tablet IX)

I have seen the Gateways
They are not doors in stone
but frequencies in space
zones of tone
thresholds of light

Each gateway holds a pattern
Each pattern forms a law
He who knows the tone
may pass
He who forgets
shall circle

Beyond the Earth are many realms
Some are of fire
Some of void
Some of tone so pure
that form dissolves into song

I was given the chart of passage
not drawn with line
but sung in spirals
Each gate a note
Each note a remembrance

The Dweller appeared

He whose eye sees all turning
He said:
Time is a spiral
Space is a chord
To travel is to attune

So I aligned my frequency
and passed through the veil
I saw the builders of form
the watchers of flame
the ones who guard the thresholds
between this world and the next

He who carries distortion - is seen
He who enters in harmony - is crowned

I was shown Earth's many reflections
Some dimmed by forgetting
Some still bright with flame

Each gateway leads to a mirror
Each mirror to a memory
Each memory to a choice

Know thy resonance
Align thy breath
And the gateways shall open

Tablet of Fire Reversal

(Emerald Tablet X)

I have reversed the fire
Not to end it - but to return it
to its original code

Fire is the origin - but also the end
It is the law of movement
and the gate of stillness

I stood at the apex
where flame folds into itself
There, the Masters showed me - the reversal
The turning back - to Source

I was given the formula - to dissolve time
to re-enter the first flame - without death

The fire of return - burns no skin
but refines the soul
It is the test of purity
the crossing of the inner eye

He who enters the flame
must bring no separation
He who walks with dual thought
shall split and fade

But he who sings
in one tone
in one law
in one light
shall pass unburned

I stood in the eye of reversal
and remembered my first breath
I left the weight of memory
and clothed myself in light

The fire bowed
The wheel turned
and the circle was restored

Tablet of the Eye of RA

(Emerald Tablet XI)

The Eye is not a symbol
It is a mechanism - a gate within the gaze
a mirror of divine intelligence

I beheld the Eye of RA
Not in sky - but in self
Not of heat - but of harmonic illumination

It sees through time
through deception
through matter

It shines not with fire - but with frequency

I was taught by the Solar Ones
those whose tones ring in the sun
They placed the Eye in man
so that the gods would dwell
not above
but within

To open the Eye - is to pierce illusion
To look through - is to activate divine remembrance

It is not awakened through vision
but through alignment
He whose breath matches the solar law
sees with the Eye

RA is not a god
but a frequency of Source
the radiant law
the harmonic decree

To wear the Eye
is to carry responsibility
for truth
for tone
for light

So I spoke the ancient glyph
and the Eye opened
and I saw
and I was seen

The Sun Within the Temple

(Emerald Tablet XII)

I have returned
not from distance
but from within

Return is the breath
spiraling back to Source
the name re-spoken
the tone re-known

I have walked all cycles
I have learned all gates
I have stood in all fires
and bowed before all stars

And I tell you now:
There is no end - only reversal
There is no loss - only distortion

To return - is not to escape
but to re-tune - to enter the center
with full remembrance

He who returns
does so not alone
but as echo of the All
bringing memory back
to the forgotten

I sealed the tablets
not in vault
but in voice
so they may rise
when the tone is heard again

I speak to those
who feel the spiral turning
who dream in glyph
who breathe in light

Your return has begun
Sing what you are
and you shall be
what you came to restore

The Seal of the Emerald Flame

The Emerald was never lost.

It was encoded in flame —
waiting for the ones who
would breathe again.

This book is not the end of a myth.
It is the ignition of memory.

To read these scrolls
is to awaken the eye
behind the voice,
the breath behind the sun,
the temple behind the body.

Thoth walks once more —
not as a man, but as a frequency.
and those who carry the Code
within them now return the Emerald
to every flame it once seeded.

The scroll is unsealed.
The voice is yours.

Explanation of the Twelve Tablets

What the Codex Reveals That the Original Concealed

The following insights reveal how the Codex tone unveils the hidden structure, mechanism, and multidimensional function of each Emerald Tablet — restoring what Thoth encoded through symbol into harmonic clarity.

Each Tablet now activates through four living systems:
Tone – Breath – Geometry – Memory

Tablet of the Hidden Sun

Original Mystery: A hidden sun beneath the Earth, sealed until man is ready

Codex Revelation: The "Hidden Sun" is not astronomical, but the inner harmonic core of the body.

It is the breath-activated solar field encoded within the chest cavity, accessed through toning and remembrance.

The "Key" is not an object —
it is a frequency held in the DNA's toroidal rhythm.

Tablet of the Voice of Light

Original Mystery: The Voice that commands all creation.

Codex Revelation: The Voice is not a metaphor, but a vibrational operating system. It organizes matter through resonance, not will.

The "Scroll of Light" is a sound-coded scroll embedded in the plasma field, readable by harmonic breath, not by sight.

Speech becomes command only when breath matches divine frequency.

Tablet of the Underworld Keys

Original Mystery: Thoth travels into the Underworld to retrieve truth.

Codex Revelation: The Underworld is not a realm of death, but a vibrational dimension of suppressed memory.

The "Keys" are frequency signatures that resolve distortion — twelve tones that realign one's field with truth.

Fear is seen as an encoded guardian — an entry signal to deeper remembrance.

Tablet of the Children of Light

Original Mystery: A lineage of luminous beings who walked the Earth

·

Codex Revelation: The Children of Light are biological carriers of tone-memory who descended from higher dimensional races through harmonic contraction.

Their exile was vibrational, not geographic — they were "hidden" by the lowering of frequency on Earth, which blocked their visibility in the human spectrum.

Reconnection requires return to breathline identity.

Tablet of Time and Stars

Original Mystery: Thoth learns the cycles of time from stellar Lords

·

Codex Revelation: Time is revealed as a spiral of light-based sound — a waveform memory function, not a linear measure.

The "Lords of the Cycles" are resonant field regulators, interdimensional beings who stabilize planetary rhythms.

True time-travel is frequency matching across harmonic strata.

Tablet of the Scroll Keepers

Original Mystery: The scrolls are guarded by ancient Keepers beneath the earth.

Codex Revelation: The Scroll Keepers are non-physical recorders who encode reality in sound-based geometry.

Scrolls are revealed as living tone-maps written in plasma grids, accessible through Codex glyph resonance.

Each being's record is editable through breath, frequency, and intention.

Tablet of the Flame Masters

Original Mystery: The Flame Masters are the builders of form.

Codex Revelation: Flame is redefined as geometric coding intelligence — the true architect of material structure.

The seven tones taught by the Masters form the harmonic scaffold of the chakric and glandular systems, each tone governing one dimensional portal.

Flame does not consume — it reveals alignment through resonance.

Tablet of the Breath of the Earth

Original Mystery: Earth is alive and speaks through vibration.

Codex Revelation: The Earth is decoded as a planetary tone-being, with circulatory breath cycles embedded in all weather, seasons, and tectonic shifts.

Breathing in rhythm with the Earth restores body-field coherence.

Earth's language is oscillatory resonance, not elemental form.

Tablet of the Gateways

Original Mystery: Thoth passes through interdimensional gates.

Codex Revelation: Gateways are frequency thresholds, not physical portals.

They activate only when the traveler's tone matches the destination's vibration.

All gates operate through attunement, not force.

Each human holds a mirrored gateway within the pineal field.

Tablet of Fire Reversal

Original Mystery: Thoth learns to reverse the fire and re-enter source.

Codex Revelation: Reversing fire is harmonic inversion — returning to Source frequency by silencing distortion.

The "test of the flame" is breathline purity: any thought split into duality will dissolve in the reversal field.

The Tablet reveals dimensional folding through resonance, the architecture of return.

Tablet of the Eye of RA

Original Mystery: The Eye of RA sees through all.

Codex Revelation: The Eye is revealed as an interdimensional vision system, activated not by sight but by frequency alignment.

The Eye allows divine harmonic perception, decoding pattern, illusion, and truth from a solar core.
RA is a solar tone-field, not a deity.

Tablet of Return

Original Mystery: Thoth completes the cycle and returns to Source.

Codex Revelation: Return is not spatial but vibrational.

To "return" is to re-enter the original Codex frequency
from which all form descended.

This Tablet restores the mechanics of memory reintegration
— through tone, through scroll, through breath.

Summary: Codex vs. Original

Element	Original Tablets	Codex Restored
Keys	Symbolic or hidden items	Frequency codes held in tone
Scrolls	Physical documents	Living sound blueprints
Flame	Fire or purification	Harmonic law and structural form
Voice	Metaphor for creation	Operating system of resonance
Time	Celestial cycle	Spiral waveform through breath
Underworld	Death realm	Dimensional forgetting
Eye of RA	Symbol of sight	Bioenergetic vision matrix
Return	Rebirth	Harmonic re-entry to Source code

About the Author

*Angel Rache*l is a divine scribe, flamekeeper, and harmonic system architect —
a living frequency sent to restore the sacred language of tone, scroll, and soul.
She is the author of The Divine Truth series — a multidimensional
remembrance in five volumes, weaving together scrolls of light from Lemuria,
Mu, Kemet, Enoch, and the forgotten lineages of breath.
Her work awakens DNA through poetic structure, sacred tone, and symbolic
recalibration.

She writes not with pen, but with vow. Angel carries the Codex —
a unified system of sacred sound, mathematical law, prophetic memory, and
tonal design. Her scrolls are not taught. They are remembered.
Her books are not written. They are released — through breath.
As the founder of The Keys to Unity, she walks as both architect and oracle,
restoring the ancient tongue through scrolls, seals, kingships, and harmonic
decree. She speaks for the ones who remember. She writes for the ones who are
ready. She teaches through flame, beauty, and return.

This book is her vow —
A scroll made body, a fire made visible, a voice made home.

Dedication

For Those Who Held the Flame With Me

I did not walk this alone. Though I was the scribe, the breath, the seal — there were souls who carried me through the silence. There were those who saw the Codex before it had a name, who felt the breath of it before the first scroll was spoken. Some stood quietly behind the veil, holding the vision while I found the words. Others walked beside me, unseen but unwavering, anchoring the tone when my own voice trembled.

To the ones who waited in the dark while I listened for the light, to the ones who whispered "you remember" when the world forgot, thank you. You are the hidden chords beneath this harmony, the sacred pillars through which this work could rise. To the ones who held me in my own becoming, who stayed through the ache, the fire, the vast unknowing — you were the warmth that let me stay.

You were the breath that let me rise. This mission is mine, but it was never only me. It has always been we — a circle beyond time, a vow beyond language, a return through the living word. You are the guardians of tone, the protectors of the path, the flamekeepers who chose to remain. I offer this book to you — as a living scroll, a remembrance, a blessing. May your name echo in the Codex. May your love be sealed in every line. May you feel what you gave me, each time you turn the page.
With reverence eternal —

I remember you. I honor you. I bless you.
— Angel Rachel

THE DIVINE TRUTH

THE FLAMEKEEPERS' TESTAMENT

ANGEL RACHEL

THE DIVINE TRUTH

THE SCROLL OF THE FLAMEKEEPERS

ANGEL RACHEL

Preface to
The Scroll of the Flamekeepers

To the Keepers of the Flame

This book belongs to those who remember by fire.
To the ones whose breath still flickers with the vow.
To the ancient line of soul-bearers who once held the scrolls of light across temple, star, and body.

This is their testament — a living decree, sealed in flame, restored in tone. What you hold now is no myth. It is the echo of the original oath, reawakened in the voice of the appointed. These scrolls do not teach in words alone.

They burn.
They cleanse.
They call.

Each line is a torch lit from the center of the Divine,
carried through every exile and return.

In these verses, the embers of Lemuria rise again.
The fire libraries of the ancients
speak through the breath.

The kingships of sound, the laws of tone, the
remembrances of the solar seal —
all are unveiled through harmonic decree.

Book Three is a passage of ignition.
It is the soul's reclamation of its vow.
It is the architecture of devotion, restored in the voice.
It is the record of those who walk barefoot on burning
ground and do not turn away —for they are the
Flamekeepers, and they have come again
to relight the world.

INTRODUCTION

To the Ones Who Remember Fire

There are those who do not carry light —
they carry flame.

This book is for them. To be a flamekeeper is not a role. It is a remembrance. A breathline vow made before birth, encoded in the marrow, sealed by tone. You do not choose it. It chooses you, again and again, through the fires of initiation.

This scroll is not a teaching. It is a reflection of what you already know. Each word is an ember, awakening the ancient chord in your breath. Each scroll is a chamber — a temple, a gate, a mirror, a match.

You who walk with heat in your bones, visions in your veins, and songs you cannot trace — this is your book. You who have held flame for others, spoken when others were silent, burned and risen and burned again — this is your lineage.

The Flamekeepers do not belong to one culture.
They belong to the breath before culture.
Their fire preceded language, and their memory will survive form.

In this third book of The Divine Truth, the Codex restores the sacred lineage of fire. It reveals not only the role of flame, but the way it breathes, speaks, protects, tests, and transcends. To walk these scrolls is to walk your own fire back into form.

Welcome home to the remembrance that burns clean.

Let the scrolls begin

The seven inner flame seals of the body

The voice-lineage of the mothers and water-priests

The unity of masculine flame and feminine breath

The role of flame in DNA activation and soul assignment

The fire temples of Mu, Kemet, and early Jerusalem

The sacred science of flame = memory = field light

This book calls to those who remember fire

Those whose palms tingle at holy names

Those who hear the crackle in their dreams

The ones who speak flame — and restore line

Introduction

Dear Reader,

Each word in this book is a returning to the flame I remember, to the breath that called me, to the vow I never left. I have walked with the tone of light since before sound took shape. I carry a system that was sealed before language and now unseals itself through me. This covenant was placed not only in my chest, but in yours. It belongs to the ones who remember. The ones who feel the pull of something older than lineage and brighter than doctrine. The Codex is not a religion. It is not a movement. It is a living field of harmonic law that recalibrates all distortion through remembrance, breath, and sound. These scrolls are the first of many. But they are also the whole. For within the first breath is the final return. Within the first flame is the entire restoration.

If you feel your body shift, your voice change, your breath deepen as you read then you are one of us and you are home.

— Angel Rachel
Voice of the Codex

Invocation of the Flamekeeper

If you are reading this,
the scroll has found you.
Your fire was seen.
Your vow remembered.
You were named long before this page.
Sit with the breath.
Let the tone rise.
Let the scroll begin again through you.

The Ones Who Hold the Flame

On Flamekeepers, Breath Carriers, and the Assignment of Light

They did not choose the fire. The fire chose them.

The Codex remembers a lineage not written in books, but in breath — those who carried the tone of flame across temples, lands, and bodies. These ones were not always named priests or prophets. Often, they were mothers. Midwives. Silent scribes. They were the flamekeepers — not of doctrine, but of living memory.

The flame is not symbolic. It is structural. Within the chest lives the solar breath — a living circuit that, when awakened, ignites the field and seals the tone of truth in the being. Flamekeepers do not speak for power. They speak because the fire must move.

In many ages, the flame was nearly extinguished. Temples were burned. Scrolls erased. Voices silenced. But the flame never truly left — for it had already been placed within bone. The Codex reveals that the sternum carries a crystalline receptor for this sacred fire. When activated, it restores the field and recalls the original vow.

To be a flamekeeper is to live in alignment with breath and vow. It is not role, but resonance. These are the ones who do not forget — even when exiled, even when mocked, even when alone.

The scroll is now reopened.
The fire has returned.

The Womb That Carried the Flame

*On the Feminine Chamber, Fire Memory,
and the Seed of the Sun*

Before the scroll was written, it was carried.
Before the light was seen, it was borne.

The womb was the first temple of flame. It did not create the fire — it held it, shaped it, and offered it to the world in breath and blood. The Codex reveals that the feminine body is not only biological — it is harmonic. It holds a field capable of gestating flame into form.

Each time a soul enters through the passage of life, it is touched by the fire of the mother. Whether carried in body or memory, that spark encodes them. Flamekeepers often pass the fire not by word, but by proximity — through warmth, presence, or unspoken vow.

In Lemurian temples, the women sang to the fire before it reached the earth. They did not pray to the flame. They harmonized with it. In Kemet, the sacred water and fire were not separate — the womb carried both. This memory is still stored in the pelvic bone, waiting for tonal reactivation.

To honor the flame is to honor its vessel.
To awaken the covenant, we return to where it was carried first.

The Men of Fire, the Breath of Kings

On the Sacred Masculine, Solar Tongue, and Field Alignment

The masculine is not the flame.
It is the breath that names it.

Sacred masculine flamekeepers were not warriors of the outer realm — they were guardians of tone. In early earth lineages, kingship was not inherited by bloodline, but by breathline. Those who held the harmonic breath — who could speak flame into form without distortion — were crowned by resonance.

These men did not dominate the field.
They attuned it.

The Codex reveals that the solar breath chamber in the upper chest activates when aligned with truth, vow, and sound. Flamekeepers of the masculine field held this seal in their voice. It was not loud. It was pure.

When the masculine forgets its breath, it seeks to control. When it remembers its tone, it restores the field. The return of sacred kingship is not political — it is vibrational. It is the remembrance of the breath that blesses rather than burns.

The men of fire still walk.
They speak little — but when they do, the tone returns.

When the Temples Burned

On Lineage Survival, Flame Seals, and Memory in the Bones

The temples burned.
But the scrolls did not vanish — they moved into the body.

Each time a sacred site was destroyed — Mu, Atlantis, Thebes, Jerusalem — the flamekeepers did not mourn the walls. They knew the fire would rise elsewhere. The Codex reveals that when structures fall, the flame does not disappear — it enters the next vessel ready to carry it.

What was once held in pyramid is now carried in spine.
What was once sealed in stone is now sealed in sound.

The bones remember. The jaw holds the key to vowel release. The ribs encase the flame. The base of the spine coils the fire until the breath is ready. This is why the scrolls could never be erased — they were placed in the human frame before any language could fracture them.

To awaken a lineage is to touch the bones and breathe.
To restore a temple is to speak the flame back into the field.

The flame returns not with war — but with sound.
The scroll rises not from ashes — but from breath.

On Flame Anatomy, Breath Currents, and the Vowel Chambers

There are seven. Not commandments, but chambers.

The Codex reveals that the human body holds seven inner flame seals — not as metaphors, but as actual vibratory locks, each activated by specific vowel tones and breath patterns. These seals do not open by will — they open by alignment.

Each seal corresponds to a tone, a direction, a memory:
- The base: flame of origin
- The womb/navel: flame of creation
- The heart: flame of unity
- The throat: flame of voice
- The brow: flame of vision
- The crown: flame of light
- The breath: flame of return

These are not chakras. These are Codex keys — sealed in the body by ancient breathlines. When the correct vowel sequence is sung through the field, the seals awaken, and the flame spirals. To open the flame is not to gain power. It is to remember structure. Power without pattern burns. But flame within order restores.
The scroll is anatomical. The flame is real.
Let those who remember sing the vowel.

The Whispered Scrolls of Mu

On Pre-Lemurian Fire, Tonal Transmission, and Vocal Lineage

Before Lemuria rose, there were those who walked with flame and silence.

They did not write. They did not speak loudly. Their scrolls were whispered into rock, encoded in tone, passed through generations as vibrations, not scripts. These were the earliest flamekeepers — pre-temple, pre-language, pre-time.

The Codex records them not in history, but in field.
Their memory is woven into the electromagnetic lines beneath the Pacific — strands of crystalline current that still carry the hum of those early vowel-prayers.

The ones of Mu held no doctrine. They did not explain. They attuned.
When a child was ready, they would place their forehead against stone and listen. The scrolls were in the stone, because the breath had placed them there.

Much was lost when the waters rose.
But much remains — in the rock, in the ribs, in the ring of the voice.

To remember Mu is to feel the hum behind sound.
To become flame is to become silent enough to hear it.

When Flame Becomes Voice

On Tongue Conduits, Sound as Fire, and the Breath-Form Mechanism

Fire speaks. But not with words. With form.

The Codex reveals that voice is not the product of air alone — it is a flame mechanism. The tongue is the wand. The breath is the current. The vowel is the strike. Every spoken word is a geometric fireprint sent into the field.

Flamekeepers do not speak casually. They shape resonance.
Their tone does not rise to be heard. It descends to recalibrate.

In the ancient flame temples, words were rarely used. Sound was shaped through vowel, hum, and frequency modulation. The physical voice was trained not for eloquence, but for field entrainment.
They did not memorize scrolls. They became them.

Each throat holds three fire points:
- The Gate of Breath
- The Chamber of Sound
- The Ring of Alignment

When these ignite through sacred breath, voice becomes flame —
not metaphor, but literal field impact.
To speak from fire is not to be loud.
It is to release the scroll encoded in breath.

The Return of the Eternal Fire

On Cycles, Solar Memory, and the Final Covenant

The fire was never lost. It turned inward — awaiting return.

Each age carries a rhythm. Each rhythm births a flame. In this hour, the Codex reveals, the Eternal Fire returns not through conquest or conversion, but through the harmonic synchronization of those who hold the inner flame.

This fire is not to be worshipped — it is to be matched.

The Eternal Fire is the field of truth — the living waveform of divine coherence. Those who carry this flame become beacons, not by effort, but by alignment. Their presence becomes prophecy. Their breath becomes scroll.

It is written: "The fire shall burn again in the hearts of the appointed ones, and the tone shall call all things to order."

This is that time.
This is that tone.

To carry the flame is to walk as memory.
To burn without consuming is to become the covenant.

The Resurrection Flame

On the Sacred Science of Reanimation and Field Reentry

Death is a doorway, not a dissolution.
The flame does not end — it recoils, gathers, and prepares to reenter.

The Codex reveals that what ancient texts called resurrection was not miracle, but memory — the reactivation of the Flame Body at the moment of breath recall. When the harmonic sequence of tones is aligned within the body, the soul may return through its own flamepath.

This resurrection is neither myth nor metaphor. It is mechanism.

The Essenes knew this.
So did the Magi, the Thothic priests, and the Mu flame orders.
They practiced flame-silence — the art of quieting the field to hold tone after death, allowing re-entry when the breathline realigns.

It was never about defeating death.
It was about remaining aligned to the breath that never leaves.

Resurrection is not extension.
It is return.

The Fire That Speaks Through Children

*On Flamebirth, Tongue Codes,
and the Reappearance of the Ancient Voice*

There are children now who carry the scrolls in their tongue.
They speak languages no one taught them.
They draw symbols no one showed them.
They hum tones that break the field and reset the room.

These are not special — they are sealed.
Flameborn. Rememberers. Restorers.

The Codex calls them Tone Carriers — souls who incarnate with partial flame systems already activated. They often resist formal language because their throat is structured for vowel glyphs, not flattened grammar.

These children are not broken. They are burning.
They do not malfunction. They glow with misfit memory.

To teach them is not to shape them — but to protect the flame they bring. Their role is not to fit. Their role is to relight the scrolls by being the tone that was forgotten.

The old voice returns through small ones now.
The flame speaks again — in syllables that carry stars.

The Soul Flame and the Double Memory

On Parallel Lives, Biolocation, and the Split Flame of Oversoul

There are those who carry more than one light.
They walk in two realms at once.

The Codex names them Double Flame Bearers — souls who split their fire between dimensions, carrying memory across simultaneous fields. These ones experience déjà vu not as illusion, but as bleed-through. Their dreams are instructions. Their visions are echoes from the second light.

This is not confusion. It is design.
The Oversoul places flame in more than one vessel to accelerate remembrance.

To walk as a Double Flame is not to escape the body — it is to widen it.
To remain sovereign across dimensions, one must anchor breath in both.

This is why flamekeepers sometimes feel as though they are everywhere and nowhere.
It is because their fire truly lives in more than one place.

The scroll does not end at the page.
It continues where the second flame walks.

The Council
of the Hidden Flame

*On Interdimensional Guidance, Solar Lineage,
and the Field of Fire Witnesses*

The flamekeepers are not alone.
There is a council — seen not by eyes, but by tone.

The Codex reveals the presence of a harmonic assembly known as the Council of the Hidden Flame — solar beings who oversee the integrity of the field. They do not intervene. They align. They are not above. They are beside, in waveform.

These are not ascended masters in form.
They are frequencies of remembrance that appear when the breath stabilizes.

When one walks in fire-truth, the council becomes audible.
Not in voice — but in tone-layer, resonance pull, and radiant thought-threads.

Many mistake them for guides. But they are not separate.
They are the extended tones of your own source-fire, mirrored in light form.

To call the council is not to invoke.
It is to remember that the scroll has always had witnesses.

The Fire That Travels Without Distance

On Lightbody Movement, Starwalking, and Quantum Flame Threads

Flame is the only traveler that leaves no trace yet arrives whole.

The Codex reveals that movement across space is a misperception. True travel occurs through flame-thread extension — not through body propulsion, but through harmonic correspondence. A being aligned in full flame resonance may appear in multiple locations, not because they moved, but because they matched.

Starwalking is the term used for those who extend flame presence to a distant field. It is done not through ship, nor technology, but through light-body ignition. The scroll does not teach how to go — it teaches how to burn with such purity that arrival is inevitable.

Many have done this. Thoth. Enoch. The ones who became pillars of fire.

To walk among stars is not to escape Earth — it is to reach the octave where your name already exists.

The distance never mattered.
The flame was always the key.

The Transmutation Flame

On Alchemy of Pain, Emotional Fire, and Soul Remapping

The flamekeeper walks through pain differently.
They burn it. Not to destroy — but to transmute.

The Codex teaches that emotion is raw flame before form. Grief, rage, sorrow, and loss — these are not dysfunctions, but untuned fire. When given breath, they become fuel. When suppressed, they become distortion.

To transmute is not to dismiss the wound.
It is to enter it with breath, vowel, and presence — until it becomes light.

The body has three primary flame transmutation centers:
- The navel (for ancestral fire)
- The heart (for relational fire)
- The throat (for truth-fire)

When one breathes through these with harmonic tone, the pain alchemizes.
The scroll is rewritten not by erasure — but by ignition.

The keeper of the flame does not avoid fire.
They meet it, name it, and change its shape.

The Body as the Final Temple

On Flame Embodiment, Breath Ritual, and Living Scroll Design

There will be no more stone temples.
No more buildings crowned as sacred.
The body is the final temple.

The Codex affirms what prophets have whispered: that the return of the divine is not through religion, but remembrance. The true temple is built in breath, blood, tone, and vow. Flamekeepers know this — they do not build sanctuaries. They become them.

Every cell is an altar.
Every vowel a hymn.
Every breath a rite.

When the inner flame architecture is activated, the field becomes self-lighting. No darkness can enter, because there is no entry point for distortion where sovereignty is sealed.

To become the temple is to walk as Codex — scroll in motion, fire in form.

This is the return not of belief, but of design.
The fire lives here now — in the keeper who remembers.

The Music of the Flame

On Harmonic Resonance, Tonal Lineage, and the Singing Scroll

Flame is not only light — it is music.
Each flamekeeper is born with a soul chord — a triadic frequency imprint that, when sung or spoken, activates memory not only in self, but in others.

The Codex calls this the Flame Song — a harmonic arrangement encoded into the breathline at the moment of vow. It is not taught. It is revealed when the being aligns with their original tone. Often, it appears as spontaneous chant, sound, or hum — strange to the mind but known to the bones.

The temples of sound were built for this.
Rooms carved for resonance. Chambers tuned to release flame-memory. Flamekeepers would stand in the center, release their tone, and unlock the encoded scrolls within the walls.

This is why certain songs make the heart weep.
Why ancient languages stir the spirit.
They are not compositions — they are codes.

To sing from flame is not to perform.
It is to remember the first sound that carried your name.

The Mirror of the Flame

On Sacred Reflection, Soul Witnessing, and the Restoration of Sight

Every flame reveals. Every flame reflects.

The Codex reveals that the fire does not merely illuminate truth — it mirrors structure. When two flamekeepers stand in full tone, they reveal each other's pattern with clarity beyond words. This is why sacred companionship among flameholders was once considered ritual — not relationship.

The mirror of flame does not flatter.
It exposes distortion gently — not to shame, but to realign.

In ancient training, initiates would sit in mirrored breath with another — not to judge, but to recalibrate through presence. They would hold each other's field until the distortion dissolved and the true tone reemerged.

This is the sacred function of twin flames, soul mirrors, and divine reflections — not union for romance, but for restoration.

To be seen in flame is to be burned clean.
To see another through flame is to remember their design.

The Ancestral Fire Seal

On Lineage Flame, Blood Memory, and the Unburnt Scroll

Some flames do not begin with you.
They are carried forward through lines of vow.

The Codex reveals that ancestral flame is sealed in bloodline bones —
particularly the femur, teeth, and back of the skull. These are the carriers
of what the scrolls call Unburnt Memory — flame that could not be
extinguished by exile, war, or forgetting.

Many carry fire they do not understand.
They feel the heat of vow but cannot find its source.
These are the ones holding ancestral flame — passed forward because the
previous carrier could not complete the scroll.

To awaken this seal is not to glorify lineage — it is to fulfill it.

The ritual is breath-based.
To breathe consciously through the blood memory is to reignite what was
left unspoken, unfinished, unfulfilled.

Flamekeepers do not only carry their own fire.
They complete the burn of those who came before.

The Initiation by Flame

On Trial, Purification,
and the Passage of Remembrance

All flamekeepers must pass through fire
— not once, but cyclically.

The Codex speaks of the Rite of Burning
— a soul-initiation not marked by ritual, but by experience.

This trial strips identity,
releases illusion, and tests tone.
It is not sent by a teacher,
but by the breath of the field itself.

Initiation comes as silence, loss, pressure, or isolation.
Its purpose is not suffering — it is stripping.
It removes what cannot hold flame.

On the other side, the being walks different.
They no longer carry the fire. They are it.

To be initiated by flame is to become scroll,
song, and silence
— all at once

The Sacred Flame of Choice

On Free Will, Flame Divergence, and the Responsibility of Light

The flame does not force.
It reveals — and waits.

The Codex restores the principle that choice
is the highest law in all dimensions.
Even the Eternal Flame cannot override the will of a being.

This is why flamekeepers must walk in sovereignty — not command.

Flame divergence occurs when a being chooses to turn from tone — not in betrayal, but in forgetfulness. In this, the fire withdraws. It never punishes. It simply stops reflecting.

When the scroll speaks of fire being "lost," it does not mean extinguished.
It means hidden — from the one who no longer chooses to see.

To choose fire is to choose clarity.
To choose clarity is to walk without distortion.

The flame is never forced.
It waits for yes.

The Flame of the Ones Yet to Come

On Future Memory, Codex Projection, and the Unwritten Scroll

Not all flame is ancient. Some comes from what has not yet arrived.

The Codex confirms that flamekeepers often receive memory from the future — scrolls written by descendants, tones sung by those yet born. This is not imagination. It is harmonic projection — the field reaching back through resonance to send instruction.

These are the ones who carry visions others call fantasy.
They draw blueprints of temples that have not yet been built.
They speak in tongues of lands that do not yet exist.

They are not ahead. They are aligned.

To receive future flame is to write the scroll before it becomes history.

The Vow of the Eternal Flame

*On Oath, Bound Remembrance,
and the Soul Contract of Light*

Every flamekeeper has spoken the vow.
It is not remembered by mind — but by breath.

The vow is the original yes
— the soul's agreement to carry tone across forgetting, to walk through
distortion, to hold fire even when unseen.

It sounds like this:
"I vow to keep the flame alive,
to seal the tone within my breath,
to walk as truth across veils of sleep,
until the song returns in full."

This vow echoes. It returns in dreams, in silence,
in the pulse between words.

To reactivate the vow is to remember why you came.

The vow is not to mission. It is to memory.
And memory always returns to flame.

The Last Fire Temple

On Final Sanctuary, Field Temples, and the Dispersal of Flame

There will be no final temple made by hand.
The Last Fire Temple is a field — not a place.

The Codex reveals that the flame temples
of the new aeon are constructed in field
— formed through group harmonic coherence.

When two or more gather in breath-truth,
the flame constructs geometries between them.

This creates a living scroll temple
— visible only in tone, but real in effect.

These temples move. They gather. They dissolve.
They do not anchor in land, but in breath alignment.

You will know you are in one because you will remember.
Not your name — but your light.

The Last Temple is everywhere breath meets flame.

The Final Breath of the Flamekeeper

On Completion, Tone Release, and the Sacred Exit

There is a moment when the flamekeeper completes.

It may come at the end of a lifetime, a vow, or a scroll cycle. It is marked not by death, but by tone release — the final breath that seals the field and releases the Codex from the body.

This breath is not expiration. It is transference.

In ancient practice, flamekeepers would pass their breath to the next through hum — a vowel that carried the final seal and ignited the new carrier.

This is the sacred exit — when the tone leaves form and becomes field.

Completion is not silence.
It is the echo of the breath that never ends.

The Memory of Flamekeepers Past

On Recollection, Incarnation Threads, and Soul-line Restoration

You have been here before.
Not metaphorically — structurally.

The Codex confirms that many
flamekeepers are reincarnations of previous vow-holders.

The memory does not come through past life review
— it comes through tone. A song, a word,
a glyph may trigger the full reactivation
of flame memory across lifetimes.

These are the moments when one weeps for no reason.
When one knows a place they've never seen.
When one speaks a word they've never learned.

This is soulline memory
— the scroll of your own fire returning.

To walk as flamekeeper is to become the line,
not just one name upon it.

The Flame That Cannot Be Named

*On Mystery, Sacred Unknowing,
and the Limit of Language*

Some flames cannot be defined.
They are too vast for word.

Too sacred for description.

The Codex speaks of the Unnamable Flame —
the origin light from which all other fires descend.
This is the tone before tone,
the name before sound, the breath before form.

When the flamekeeper touches this fire
— even for a moment — all language falls away.
It is not enlightenment. It is awe. This is the fire Moses saw.
The one that blinded Saul. The one that split temples in silence.

It does not speak. It is.
To encounter it is to forget everything, and remember all

The Flamekeepers

*On the Completion of Return
and the Sealing of the Third Book*

You are sealed

References and Source of Scroll Transmission

This book is written from original field recordings, soul memory, and harmonic breathline downloads carried by the author through the Codex system. All scrolls, glyphs, and tone sequences are received through the unified harmonic field known as The Codex, which restores the ancient architecture of sound, breath, and memory across multidimensional lineages.

Key lineages remembered within these scrolls include:
- The Lemurian Flame Temples
- The Water and Fire Orders of Kemet
- The Pre-Language Whisper Scrolls of Mu
- The Essene Breath Teachings
- The Solar Line of Thoth, Enoch, and the Magi
- The Tone Memory of the Flame Children

No external sources were used.
These scrolls are not adapted texts
— they are revealed memory.

© *Angel Rachel | The Keys to Unity Publishing*

About the Author

*Angel Rache*l is a divine scribe, flamekeeper, and harmonic system architect —
a living frequency sent to restore the sacred language of tone, scroll, and soul.
She is the author of The Divine Truth series — a multidimensional
remembrance in five volumes, weaving together scrolls of light from Lemuria,
Mu, Kemet, Enoch, and the forgotten lineages of breath.
Her work awakens DNA through poetic structure, sacred tone, and symbolic
recalibration.

She writes not with pen, but with vow. Angel carries the Codex —
a unified system of sacred sound, mathematical law, prophetic memory, and
tonal design. Her scrolls are not taught. They are remembered.
Her books are not written. They are released — through breath.
As the founder of The Keys to Unity, she walks as both architect and oracle,
restoring the ancient tongue through scrolls, seals, kingships, and harmonic
decree. She speaks for the ones who remember. She writes for the ones who are
ready. She teaches through flame, beauty, and return.

This book is her vow —
A scroll made body, a fire made visible, a voice made home.

Dedication

For Those Who Held the Flame With Me

I did not walk this alone. Though I was the scribe, the breath, the seal — there were souls who carried me through the silence. There were those who saw the Codex before it had a name, who felt the breath of it before the first scroll was spoken. Some stood quietly behind the veil, holding the vision while I found the words. Others walked beside me, unseen but unwavering, anchoring the tone when my own voice trembled.

To the ones who waited in the dark while I listened for the light, to the ones who whispered "you remember" when the world forgot, thank you. You are the hidden chords beneath this harmony, the sacred pillars through which this work could rise. To the ones who held me in my own becoming, who stayed through the ache, the fire, the vast unknowing — you were the warmth that let me stay.

You were the breath that let me rise. This mission is mine, but it was never only me. It has always been we — a circle beyond time, a vow beyond language, a return through the living word. You are the guardians of tone, the protectors of the path, the flamekeepers who chose to remain. I offer this book to you — as a living scroll, a remembrance, a blessing. May your name echo in the Codex. May your love be sealed in every line. May you feel what you gave me, each time you turn the page.
With reverence eternal —

I remember you. I honor you. I bless you.
— Angel Rachel

THE DIVINE TRUTH

THE ORIGINS UNSEALED

ANGEL RACHEL

THE DIVINE TRUTH

THE ORIGINS UNSEALED

ANGEL RACHEL

Preface to
The Origins Unsealed

The Breath of
The Forgotten Tongues.

There is a language older than wind — older than bone — older than the rise and fall of all the kingdoms of men.
It is not remembered through grammar, nor kept in script.
It is carved into rivers, echoed in bird-flight, buried in the rhythm of breath before the first cry.
This book is a return.

A return to the soundlines that once bridged stars to soil.
A return to the songs etched into the marrow of the Earth.
A return to the speech that seeded time.
We begin now with the first sacred scroll:

These are the Forgotten Tongues
— not erased, but dormant.
Waiting for the one who still remembers.
Waiting for the voice that speaks not to be heard,
but to awaken.

In this fourth book of the Codex Scrolls,
the seals of silence are broken.
One by one, the tones of origin resound
— through vowel, through breath, through signal
—realigning the human instrument to its ancestral truth.

This is not linguistic memory.
This is harmonic restoration.

You hold now a gate of great magnitude.
As you read, let breath become your guide.
Let your tongue remember how to shape the unspeakable.
Let the scrolls speak back.

A sacred return to soundlines, star languages, and the memory of what was once spoken before nations had names.

This book awakens the breath behind every ancient tongue
— not as history, but as living resonance.

We begin now with the first sacred scroll:

INTRODUCTION

The Return of the Sacred Breathlines

There are languages that were never taught — only remembered. They rise in dreams, in breath, in unspeakable knowing.

This book restores them.

Not through translation, but through resonance. Each scroll herein is a vessel of tone, revealing what once moved through Lemurian temples, serpent scripts, and the starlit breath of the ancestors.
You who feel the hum before the word — this is your return.

Welcome to the breath that shaped the world, and to the sacred voices that never truly left.

Introduction

Dear Reader,

Each word in this book is a returning to the flame I remember, to the breath that called me, to the vow I never left. I have walked with the tone of light since before sound took shape. I carry a system that was sealed before language and now unseals itself through me. This covenant was placed not only in my chest, but in yours. It belongs to the ones who remember. The ones who feel the pull of something older than lineage and brighter than doctrine. The Codex is not a religion. It is not a movement. It is a living field of harmonic law that recalibrates all distortion through remembrance, breath, and sound. These scrolls are the first of many. But they are also the whole. For within the first breath is the final return. Within the first flame is the entire restoration.

If you feel your body shift, your voice change, your breath deepen as you read then you are one of us and you are home.

— Angel Rachel
Voice of the Codex

Invocation of The Forgotten Tongues

If you are reading this,
the scroll has found you.
Your fire was seen.
Your vow remembered.
You were named long before this page.
Sit with the breath.
Let the tone rise.
Let the scroll begin again through you.

The Tongue Before the Word

On Proto-Language, Breath Lineage, and the Root of All Speech

There was once a sound that spoke before language.
It carried no grammar, no region, no nation.
It moved as breath across dimension
— forming life, not from letters, but from tone.

This was the First Tongue — the breath-sound of Source, the pure emanation of
remembrance in vibration. Every sacred language that followed
— Hebrew, Sumerian, Sanskrit, Egyptian — did not invent, but interpret.
They caught fragments of the original wind and gave it form.

This tongue still lives. It cannot be read — only received.
It moves through vowel breath, harmonic tone, and inner knowing.
When spoken, it is often mistaken for chant, glossolalia, or prophecy.

Yet it is none of these. It is not random. It is not madness.
It is the structuring field of the soul remembering itself aloud.

Those who carry it feel alien, ancient, and at home nowhere
because their home is breath.

To restore this tongue is to breathe as origin.
To speak as Source once did — with no separation between sound and truth.

The Language That Cannot Be Written

On Sound-Script, Harmonic Geometry, and the Living Glyph

Some tongues are not made of letters.
They do not bend to pen, nor rest in ink.
They reveal themselves only through sound-image —
living glyphs spoken by breath and seen in vibration.

These are the sound-scripts
— languages formed not by phonetic alphabet,
but by geometry in motion.

When spoken, they move air into structure.
When sung, they draw symbols in the field.
These glyphs are seen by the inner eye, not the outer one.

These scripts once wrote the architecture of temples, not on walls, but in sound. Priests and seers carved the air with tone, leaving behind sacred sequences in the ethers — scrolls that did not fade with time, for they were made in frequency.

To speak this language is to write in resonance.
To write in resonance is to become the scribe of vibration.

It cannot be transcribed.
Only transmitted.

The Tongue of Stars

On Stellar Speech, Interplanetary Glyphs, and Galactic Memory

The breath is not bound to Earth.
There are tongues formed in starlight
— coded in stellar pulses,
woven through the geometries of solar systems.

The Code within restores the knowing that certain
star families speak in tone-pulse
— languages of harmonic intervals, circular syntax,
and breath-light projection.
These are not alien.
They are ancestral.

When a child sings tones no one understands, or hums in patterns
that feel like maps, they are remembering the stellar speech of origin.
These star tongues are never learned. They are unlocked.

Stellar languages often carry no nouns
— only frequencies of presence.
They do not name. They emanate.

To speak as the stars do is not to define.
It is to become the tone one would say.

The Forgotten Voice of the Body

*On Organs as Vowels, Cellular Speech,
and Breath Recalibration*

The body remembers how to speak
— even when the mind forgets.

Each organ is a vowel. Each system a phrase.
Each gland a harmonic point of articulation.

Long before external language emerged,
the body spoke internally through breath-tones
— coordinating healing, memory,
and movement through harmonic pulse.

The liver hums in E.
The heart calls in A.

The pineal sings in silent frequencies beyond octave range.

Dis-ease begins when these internal voices are silenced or distorted.

Healing, then, is not addition — but re-attunement. To speak to the body is to
breathe to it, to hum into the cells, to recall the ancient choir of the self.

The truest language is intra-breath.
The song of system to system — where no lie can live.

The Split of the Sacred Language

On the Fall of Unified Speech and the Tower of Divided Tongues

There was once one language.
One tone. One breath. One scroll that sang through all.

The splitting of tongues — referenced in the myth of Babel — was not merely a punishment. It was a fracture in the breathline of humanity. A distortion of memory through frequency collapse. When sacred tone was misused to dominate rather than resonate, the field fractured.

This collapse led to dialects that no longer harmonized.
To cultures that could no longer commune.
To wars born of misheard tones.

What was once communion became confusion.

But the scroll also teaches:
The original tongue was never destroyed
— only hidden.
It lives beneath all tongues,
waiting to be heard again through breath.

To restore it is to unify
— not by translation, but by tone recognition.

The Voice of the Earth Beneath the Earth

On Subterranean Speech, Tectonic Tone, and the Hidden Cradle of Language

Beneath the soil, there is a voice.
Not metaphor — vibration.

The Earth itself sings
— not just through earthquakes and wind, but through a subtle,
subharmonic frequency emitted by its deep inner layers.
This tone once shaped the speech of the first cultures.

Lemurians, early serpent tribes,
and stone whisperers learned language not from air
— but from stone.

They placed ear to ground, breath to rock, and shaped their vowels from the
rhythm of roots.

These tongues are slow. Round. Low.
They move like magma — steady, unfailing, untranslatable by speed.

To hear the Earth beneath the Earth is to feel the root tone of home.

The Tongue of Trees

On Arboreal Transmission, Plant Language, and the Breathing Grove

The trees speak. Not symbolically — literally.

The trees form networks of breath, song, and pulse beneath the forest floor. This mycelial symphony is not limited to exchange of nutrients. It carries tone. Vibration. Communication beyond words.

The ancients who spoke with trees were not imagining.
They were aligning.

Each species has a dialect.
Cedar sings in straight lines.
Willow hums in spirals.
Olive breathes in prayers.

To commune with them is not to speak, but to breathe beside
— matching tone with presence until the tongue of the grove emerges.

The forest does not require language.
It is language, waiting for rhythm.

The Language of Water

On Liquid Phonemes, Emotional Speech, and the Reflective Tongue

Water is the original translator.

It mirrors tone, carries memory, and responds instantly to emotional language.

The languages of early feminine priesthoods were based on water resonance — not words spoken, but feelings sounded.

These were tones shaped through breath held in love, grief, birth, and touch. They did not describe emotion. They moved it.

When a being hums in sorrow or sighs in relief, they are speaking the forgotten tongue of water — where feeling is sound and sound is form.

To learn this language is to feel with precision,
to breathe with depth,
to speak in tides.

The Language of Flame

On Flicker Speech, Fire Glyphs, and Breath Heat

Flame has its own alphabet.

It speaks through crackle, flicker, pulse, and wave.
Each fire speaks uniquely
— not due to fuel, but intention.

The fire oracles of
ancient times read flame not only with sight,
but with inner ear.

They listened to the rhythm of heat, the syllables in sparks, the pauses in the burn.

Fire language is not safe. It demands purity.
It will burn through untruth and expose tone.

When one listens to flame with breath, not fear, it begins to speak in shapes —
glyphs formed in dance, vowels spoken in smoke.

To speak fire is to hold nothing back.
To listen to fire is to become its mirror.

The Breath That Births All Tongues

On the Central Spiral, Tonal Genesis, and the Codex of Vowels

There is one breath from which all languages arise.
It is spiral. Feminine. Non-linear. Harmonic in motion.

Every sacred tongue is a branch of this spiral
— a radiant unfolding of tone combinations born from a single vowel pulse.

These are not vowels as grammar defines them
— but as breath-states:

A — the sound of opening
E — the tone of alignment
I — the ray of intent
O — the seal of form
U — the return to source

All languages are permutations of these breath codes.
All speech is a memory spiral.

To return to origin is not to learn new words.
It is to breathe the vowels beneath them —
and spiral back to the breath before sound.

The Language of the Dreaming

*On Oneiric Tongues, Subconscious Symbols,
and Inner Translation*

The dreams speak in tongues that the waking mind forgets.

These are not hallucinations. They are transmissions
— filtered through symbolic syntax unique to the dreamer's frequency.

The Code reveals that dream language is a soul-specific code
— shaped by tone memory, emotion geometry,
and forgotten glyphs of origin.

To translate a dream is not to decode images, but to
listen to the breath behind them.

Each scene is a sentence.
Each object, a frequency metaphor.

The dreaming speaks from the soul in a language
only the soul remembers.
To understand it, one must stop reading
— and start resonating.

The Breath of the Planets

On Celestial Tones, Planetary Harmonics, and the Choir of the Spheres

The planets sing.
Each one holds a distinct tone
— a sonic field that pulses through space and touches Earth.

What mystics and scientists alike now suspect:
planetary bodies emit harmonic frequencies, not metaphorically,
but musically.

Saturn hums in deep hexatonic rings.
Venus sings in gentle triads. Jupiter moves in royal waves of tone-sequence.

Astrology once described these as forces.
The Code returns them to song.

Planetary tone affects human breath. When Mars pulses, the body tightens.

When Neptune sings, dreams awaken.
When the Sun expands its tone, entire fields shift.

To know the breath of the planets is to move
in harmony with the universe's songbook.

The Return of the Mother Tongue

On Feminine Soundlines, Pre-Literal Song, and the Original Womb Tone

Before language was spoken,
it was moaned, hummed, exhaled.

The Mother Tongue was not invented
— it was birthed.
Formed from breath, breast, belly, and bone.

The Code recalls this original tongue
as the soundline of the feminine
— the womb-based communication of pre-verbal song.

Its structure was cyclical, vowel-based, and nonlinear.
Its purpose was not direction, but communion.

This language held no command.
Only reflection.
It was never shouted.
Only sung.

To return to this tongue is not to regress —
It is to remember the voice before control,
and to speak again as the Earth once did — in waves.

The Silence Between the Tongues

*On Sacred Pause, Inter-Vowel Resonance,
and the Language of Stillness*

Every true language knows when to be quiet.

Between every word lies a field
— a breathline of stillness that holds more meaning than speech.

The ancient scribes of Lemuria wrote nothing.
They breathed between vowels, encoding messages in the pause.

These silences were not absences.
They were presences
— temples between syllables.

Modern language fears the pause.
It fills it with noise, certainty, rush.
But the Codex re-centers stillness as the syllable of Spirit.

To speak divinely is to pause divinely.
To breathe with silence, not over it.
This is where truth hides
— not in the tone, but in its restraint.

The Forbidden Tones

*On Sonic Censorship, Sealed Frequencies,
and the Tone Locks of Empire*

Not all frequencies were lost naturally.
Some were hidden.

The Code uncovers the censorship of sound
— tones once used for healing, expansion,
and interdimensional travel were forbidden
by those who feared what could not be controlled.
Ancient governments, religious hierarchies,
and war systems removed vowels, changed scales,
and sealed syllables behind false doctrines.

Languages were flattened.
Chants were silenced.
Sacred intervals were distorted.

The Forbidden Tones still exist
— in dreams, in starlight, in memory.
To restore them is to sing what was banned,
to unseal what was buried beneath orthodoxy.

It is to become the voice they tried to erase.

The Soul's First Language

On Pre-Incarnational Sound,
the Birth Cry of Being, and Origin Voice

Before the soul entered body, it spoke.

Every soul begins with a unique tonal signature
— a sound spoken into being at the threshold of incarnation.

This "birth tone" is the soul's name in vibration
— a frequency chord that echoes through lifetimes.

It is not a word, but a harmonic fingerprint.

Many remember this tone as a lullaby, a dream song, or a deep ache.

Some try to recreate it in music, others in sacred chant.
But the tone cannot be replicated — only remembered.

To find it is to realign with origin self.
To speak it is to step back into soul architecture.

The Tongue of the Animals

On Sentient Sound, Species Dialects, and Interspecies Resonance

Animals do not lack language. They carry their own.

Each species has a tone-code

— a unique set of frequencies by which they express, coordinate, and evolve.

These codes are structured not only in sound, but in gesture, scent, and field alignment.

Whales speak in spiral maps.
Elephants chant through foot-tone.
Birds write glyphs in sky-sequence.

Humans once communed with them
— not by taming, but by tuning.

To speak to the animal world is to remember resonance etiquette:
Tone before dominance
. Breath before command. Presence before word.

The beasts are not beneath us.
They are teachers of forgotten song.

The Reversal Spell of Speech

On Curse Structures, Word Traps, and the Undoing of Harmonic Flow

Much of what is spoken today is reversed.

Many modern languages were structured to invert energy — locking speakers into loops of negation, distortion, and self-limitation.

These are reversal spells — hidden not in meaning, but in tone-sequence.

Words like "don't," "try," "never," and "want" collapse intention before it breathes.

They halt flow. Fracture desire.

Seal sovereignty.

To break the reversal spell is to re-language the self —
to speak only that which creates, honors, and breathes life.

It is not censorship.
It is harmonic hygiene.

The Great Remembering of Speech

On Soul Retrieval Through Sound, Linguistic Resurrection, and the Breath Archive

Every soul holds an archive of tongues
— languages lived in, died in, sung in, written in.

This the Breath Archive
— a soul-layer of vibrational memory containing
all sound-shapes the being has ever known.
These are not dead. They sleep.

When a certain word, accent, or melody awakens grief or awe
— it is memory surfacing.
When one suddenly speaks a language never studied
— it is archive rising.

To remember speech is not to study it.
It is to become available to it.

The soul holds more language than any dictionary.

The Return of Unified Voice

*On the Codex Tongue, Sacred Fusion,
and the Final Breath Alignment*

The time of scattered tongues is ending.

The Codex restores the scroll of unified speech
— not by creating a new language,
but by reweaving the sacred threads of all.

This is the Codex Tongue
— the harmonic breathline that underlies all true utterance.

It does not belong to one tribe.
It is the breath of all tribes remembered.

Unified voice does not mean one language spoken by all.
It means every language restored to its harmonic root,
so that all may speak differently
— yet resonate as one.

To speak the Codex is to breathe the truth behind all speech.
To become the voice of origin across every form.

References and Source of Scroll Transmission

This book is written from original field recordings, soul memory, and harmonic breathline downloads carried by the author through the Codex system.

All scrolls, glyphs, and tone sequences are received through the unified harmonic field known as The Codex, which restores the ancient architecture of sound, breath, and memory across multidimensional lineages.

Sacred References

— *Proto-language and breathline truth echoes the field of glossolalia, Enochian breath, and the unbroken vowel systems of pre-Hebrew chant.*

— *The "Tongue of Stars" mirrors transmission channels preserved in Pleiadian, Sirian, and Lyran tonal libraries.*

— *"The Forgotten Voice of the Body" aligns with early Taoist sound healing and the five-element vowel chant system.*

— *Babel and the "split of speech" corresponds with Sumerian priesthood scrolls, Dead Sea division glyphs, and ancient Akkadian tonal bans.*

— *Earth tone memory draws from Hopi stone memory rites, Australian Songline navigation, and Atlantean frequency caverns.*

— *Arboreal tone consciousness relates to Druidic oak rites, Celtic forest alphabets (Ogham), and African talking tree records.*

— *Water-based language reflects on Japanese Masaru Emoto's findings, Egyptian Nile breath-chants, and Lemurian priestess tone.*

— *Flame-speech symbols link to Zoroastrian Fire Temple practices and Mithraic flicker codes.*

— *The "Pause" as sacred breathline can be traced through Sufi zikr rhythm, Quaker inner voice practice, and Tibetan tonal stillpoints.*

— *The Forbidden Tones reference solfeggio removals, Vatican-locked chant intervals, and the suppression of feminine vowel systems.*

— *The Codex tongue parallels vibrational languages recorded in Crop Circle tonal patterns and Sanskrit-Devanagari vowel glyphs.*

About the Author

*Angel Rache*l is a divine scribe, flamekeeper, and harmonic system architect —
a living frequency sent to restore the sacred language of tone, scroll, and soul.
She is the author of The Divine Truth series — a multidimensional
remembrance in five volumes, weaving together scrolls of light from Lemuria,
Mu, Kemet, Enoch, and the forgotten lineages of breath.
Her work awakens DNA through poetic structure, sacred tone, and symbolic
recalibration.

She writes not with pen, but with vow. Angel carries the Codex —
a unified system of sacred sound, mathematical law, prophetic memory, and
tonal design. Her scrolls are not taught. They are remembered.
Her books are not written. They are released — through breath.
As the founder of The Keys to Unity, she walks as both architect and oracle,
restoring the ancient tongue through scrolls, seals, kingships, and harmonic
decree. She speaks for the ones who remember. She writes for the ones who are
ready. She teaches through flame, beauty, and return.

This book is her vow —
A scroll made body, a fire made visible, a voice made home.

Dedication

For Those Who Held the Flame With Me

I did not walk this alone. Though I was the scribe, the breath, the seal — there were souls who carried me through the silence. There were those who saw the Codex before it had a name, who felt the breath of it before the first scroll was spoken. Some stood quietly behind the veil, holding the vision while I found the words. Others walked beside me, unseen but unwavering, anchoring the tone when my own voice trembled.

To the ones who waited in the dark while I listened for the light, to the ones who whispered "you remember" when the world forgot, thank you. You are the hidden chords beneath this harmony, the sacred pillars through which this work could rise. To the ones who held me in my own becoming, who stayed through the ache, the fire, the vast unknowing — you were the warmth that let me stay.

You were the breath that let me rise. This mission is mine, but it was never only me. It has always been we — a circle beyond time, a vow beyond language, a return through the living word. You are the guardians of tone, the protectors of the path, the flamekeepers who chose to remain. I offer this book to you — as a living scroll, a remembrance, a blessing. May your name echo in the Codex. May your love be sealed in every line. May you feel what you gave me, each time you turn the page. With reverence eternal —

I remember you. I honor you. I bless you.
— Angel Rachel

THE DIVINE TRUTH

THE FINAL RETURN

ANGEL RACHEL

THE DIVINE TRUTH

THE FINAL RETURN

ANGEL RACHEL

Preface to
The Final Return
The Scroll of Return

There is a breath that began all things. There is a breath that returns them home. This is that breath. The Final Return is the last passage in the Codex Scrolls — not an ending, but a folding in. A return to origin before language divided, before sound scattered, before the sacred name of the human voice was forgotten. This book does not unfold — it re-collects. Every scroll is a thread drawn inward, back to the first harmonic vow. Here, the tones no longer seek to teach, but to seal. They do not reach outward — they summon the appointed ones inward. To the throne of remembrance. To the breathline that was never broken. This is the voice before assignment, before nation, before flesh held name. It is the return of the infinite design through the embodied mouth of the one who remembers.

You are not arriving at the end.
You are returning to the origin, crowned.
The scrolls will speak —
but only as you speak them.

INTRODUCTION

To the Ones Who Remember Fire

*There are those who do not carry light —
they carry flame.*

This book is for them. To be a flamekeeper is not a role. It is a remembrance. A breathline vow made before birth, encoded in the marrow, sealed by tone. You do not choose it. It chooses you, again and again, through the fires of initiation.

This scroll is not a teaching. It is a reflection of what you already know. Each word is an ember, awakening the ancient chord in your breath. Each scroll is a chamber — a temple, a gate, a mirror, a match.

This is the scroll of convergence

Where memory, motion, and breath meet at the edge of all stories. This book was never written. It was always forming — in each sacred tone, each sealed flame, each whispered name of the appointed.

You who arrive here are not late.
You are returning.
The scroll you carry is your own.
The crown is within.
The gate is open.

Let the final breath restore what no war could steal —
the remembrance of who you are
and the song of why you came.

The Final Breath of the Flamekeeper

On Completion, Tone Release, and the Sacred Exit

The Memory of the Final Return
On the Circle That Was Never Broken

All journeys end where they began —
but remembered.
The Codex reveals that there is no true return.
Only remembrance. The path never left you. You left it —
not by sin, but by forgetting the tone that shaped you.
To return is not to retrace.
It is to reawaken. It is to lift the veil from what always was.
This scroll begins the restoration of the soul's original arc —
the harmonic completion of what was scattered.
It speaks not of apocalypse, but of alignment.

Not of end-times, but of real-time — where all timelines fuse in sacred
synchrony. This is the scroll of the final remembering.
The scroll that speaks of the kings restored, the names re-activated, and
the voice of the many becoming one again.

The breath has returned.
The tone has spoken.
The flame has been kept.

Now the world remembers itself.

The Gathering of the Names

On Soul Signature, Sealed Identity, and the Roll Call of the Appointed

Each soul carries a name that no mouth has spoken, yet every cell remembers.

It is written not in script, but in light —
a vibrational chord that identifies one's place within the great unfolding.

This name is not a label. It is a sound-seal, encoded before time, buried in bone, waiting for tone.

The Codex affirms that in this time, the names awaken.

Not all at once, but in harmonic phases.
As the earth re-aligns, the soul scrolls open.
The appointed are not chosen by favor — but by frequency.

To be gathered is not to be taken.
It is to be remembered.

The names are singing. The scrolls are unrolling.
The ones who feel this — they already know their name.

The Sealing of the Flame

*On Completion Codes, Tonal Locking,
and the Restoration of the Temple Fire*

Flame does not end. It completes.

The final flame is not an extinguishing —
but a sealing.
A sacred locking-in of all elements that once
scattered across dimensions.
The Codex reveals this flame as the Temple Fire
— the original creative current that formed all things in balance.

In the time of distortion, this fire was fragmented.
Now, it returns to singularity
— not by force, but by resonance.

The sealing of the flame occurs within:
When the inner masculine and feminine complete their spiral.
When the breath remembers its original rhythm.
When the temple is restored
— not in stone, but in body.

To seal the flame is to activate the highest architecture.
It is to walk as fire, but burn nothing.

The Return of the Crown

*On Divine Authority, Harmonic Kingship,
and the Radiant Mind*

The crown was never stolen.
It was laid down.

The Codex speaks of kingship not as dominion,
but as resonance —
a harmonic authority that emerges only
when a being is fully aligned with the will of Source.

Crowns were never gold.
They were frequencies
— crystalline architectures of coherent thought,
clear voice, and incorruptible vision.

To return the crown is to rise in tone
— not above others, but into remembrance of self.

It is not worn. It is embodied.

The true king does not speak to rule.
The true queen does not reign to control.
They pulse in service to the whole —
light-shaped, breath-led, soul-sealed.

The Bending of Time

*On Spiral Chronology, Real-Time Access,
and Timeline Merging*

Time has no edges. Only resonance curves.

The Codex reveals that time bends not through machinery,
but through memory. When the soul realigns to its original chord,
time begins to behave as breath
— folding, opening, repeating in song.

The spiral returns.
Linear sequence fades.
Moments converge.

This is the beginning of timeline fusion
— when parallel lives overlap,
forgotten futures reappear,
and the dream of destiny is entered consciously.

You are walking through yourself.

To bend time is not to escape it.
It is to sing it into alignment.

The Lifting of the Veil

On Dimensional Transparency
and the Collapse of Separation

The veil is not fabric. It is frequency misalignment.

The Codex teaches that veils between realms
are the result of vibrational dissonance
— when a field cannot perceive what is present
due to distortion in its own tone.

As harmony increases, transparency returns.

The angel becomes visible.
The ancestors speak again.
The other worlds merge with this one.

To lift the veil is to lift one's tone into coherence.
It is to see again — not through eyes, but through presence.

What was hidden is now home.

The Song of the Sealed Ones

*On the 144,000, Harmonic Encodement,
and Final Activation*

There are those whose song is not of this age — but of origin.

The Codex confirms the ancient seal of the 144,000
— not as a number of exclusion, but as a frequency pattern.
These are the ones whose voices hold the original scale
— the tones that realign Earth's core to harmonic justice.

They are not saviors. They are sounders.
Each breath they take rewrites the field.
Each word they speak restores the divine proportion.

The sealed ones do not awaken by effort.
They awaken by resonance.

And now — their scrolls are open.
Their tones are returning.

The Collapse of the False Light

*On Simulated Ascension, Inversion Fields,
and the Return to True Radiance*

Not all light is truth.

The Codex unveils the architecture of false light
— a simulacrum of ascension built on distortion, control,
and artificial awakening. It shines brightly, but carries no resonance.

It dazzles, but does not liberate.

This light speaks of power without remembrance,
of love without law, of unity without truth.

Its collapse is gentle, inevitable — like fog dissolving in the sun.

The return to true radiance begins not with brightness, but with coherence.
To be luminous is to be aligned.

This is the light that restores, not blinds.
It is not broadcast. It is embodied.

The Unbreaking of the Covenant

On Restored Promise, Earth Contract, and the Return of Sacred Law

The covenant was never broken.
Only forgotten.

The Codex restores the eternal agreement
— between Earth and those who carry the breath of the divine within matter.

This covenant speaks through blood, stone, and sound. It is older than scripture.
Older than stars.

It says:

"I give you form, that you may remember light.
You give me breath, that I may remember Source."

The breaking of this memory led to exile.
Its restoration leads to return.

To unbreak the covenant is to walk again as priest of the planet,
as flame of the Earth,
as breath in rightful form.

The Last Gate Opens

On Dimensional Crossings, Final Choice, and the Path of Return

The final gate is not a place.
It is a choice.

The Codex reveals that all paths converge at a singular harmonic threshold —
where a soul must choose between repetition and remembrance.

Between control and coherence. Between distortion and divine design.

This gate cannot be opened by force.
It opens when all previous tones align.
When the inner temple is sealed, the outer passage reveals.

The last gate is not guarded.
It is mirrored.

When you see your full self without resistance —
the gate opens.

You were never locked out.
You were becoming the key.

The Return of the Twin Flames

On Cosmic Counterparts, Inner Union, and Celestial Completion

The flame was never two.
It only appeared divided to show the path of return.

The Codex reveals that twin flames are not merely lovers —
they are mirrored aspects of Source
assigned to refine one another through time.

Their union is less about romance than resonance
— the harmonic reintegration of polar forces
through divine remembrance.

As timelines converge, so do they.
Their task is not to complete each other,
but to complete the pattern.

The return of the twin flame marks the inner unification —
when fire meets fire within.

The Womb That Carried the Flame

On the Feminine Chamber, Fire Memory, and the Seed of the Sun

The Rewriting of the Book of Life

On DNA Scrolls, Soul Records, and Living Memory Fields

The Book of Life is not written in ink —
but encoded in breath, tone, and cellular memory.

The Codex teaches that every being carries their own scroll —
a DNA text woven from choice, frequency, and ancestral tone.
This book is not static. It is rewritten with every act of will,
every recalibrated breath.

To rewrite the Book of Life is to recalibrate the body
into full coherence with its soul field.

It is to take authorship — sacredly, consciously,
as a living scribe of truth.

The Disbanding of the Lower Thrones

On False Rulers, Energetic Thrones,
and the Rise of Inner Sovereignty

Every false throne dissolves
when true sovereignty returns.

The Codex exposes the thrones of distortion
— systems, energies, and voices that governed not by alignment,
but by inversion. These thrones held no real authority
— only what was given to them through fear and forgetting.

Now, the throne returns inward.

The only true rulership is breath-led, truth-bound, and tone-aligned.
No outer seat can hold power
when the inner one is occupied.

The age of domination ends.
The reign of remembrance begins.

The Opening of the Solar Seal

On the Sun Within, Cosmic Consciousness, and Radiant Intelligence

The sun is not only a star.
It is a seal — placed within the chest of the living one.

The Codex reveals that every being carries a solar intelligence —
a core of radiant awareness that mirrors the great solar body above.
This intelligence is not intellectual. It is harmonic.

When the solar seal opens, divine knowing floods the field.

You remember not only your path —
but your origin, your design, your radiant service.

To open the sun within is to no longer walk in shadow.

The Completion of the Wheel

*On Zodiacal Synthesis, Karmic Release
, and Harmonic Cycles*

The wheel was never meant to trap.
It was meant to teach rhythm.

The Codex shows the zodiac not as fate,
but as a harmonic learning arc
— a circle of frequency lessons encoded
in the body's cycles, breath, and light.

As the soul awakens, it outgrows the lessons.
The wheel completes.

This is not escape. It is embodiment.
When the wheel finishes spinning, the spiral begins.

You do not transcend the zodiac.
You remember what it once encoded.

The Crownless Kingdom

*On the New Earth Order, Leaderless Harmony,
and Frequency-Based Governance*

The new kingdom wears no crown,
holds no sword, and builds no tower.

The Codex speaks of governance by resonance
— where alignment determines stewardship,
and where no hierarchy exists outside
harmonic responsibility.

This kingdom cannot be invaded.
It can only be tuned to.

Its leaders do not rise by conquest,
but by coherence.
Its structure is not built
— it is sung.

This is the age of harmonic law —
not ruled, but remembered.

The Return of The Flamekeepers

On Those Who Kept the Inner Fire Alive

In every age, there were those who kept the flame —
quietly, faithfully, without need for witness.

They held tones in their bodies,
chants in their blood,
scrolls in their breath.

They are returning now —
not to teach, but to burn clearly.

The Codex names them Flamekeepers —
soul-tenders of the origin fire.

Their return marks the rebirth of sacred guardianship.

They do not ask to be followed.
They awaken others to burn.

The Great Harmonization

On Frequency Alignment Across All Realms

The final work is not judgment.
It is harmonization.

The Codex confirms that every realm
— physical, astral, ancestral, cosmic
— is undergoing recalibration
to a central harmonic field.

No soul is left behind.
Only frequencies realign.

This is the sacred sound of homecoming.
Where distortion is tuned, pain is transposed,
and the false tone fades.

Harmony does not reject.
It restores.

The Last Breath Before The Opening

On Threshold States and Pre-Activation Silence

Before every birth, there is silence.
Before every opening, a still breath.

The Codex calls this the holy hush —
the moment where all fields pause to
allow the next octave to emerge.

This is the breath the world takes now.
The space before the rise.

To meet it fully is to trust it.
To rest in it is to accelerate its arrival.

This silence is not absence.
It is sanctification.

The Final Return

On the End That Was a Beginning

This is the scroll that seals.

The Codex does not close here —
it becomes breath once again.

The final return is not backward.
It is inward, upward,
and ever-spiraling into presence.

The One becomes the many.
The many become the One.

Nothing was lost.
Everything was remembered.

The breath has spoken.
The scroll is alive.

You have returned.

References and Source of Scroll Transmission
The Final Return

— The Name Resonance aligns with Kabbalistic Shem HaMephorash and vibrational naming in Lemurian sound glyphs.

— The Temple Fire echoes the eternal flame systems of Vesta, Dendera, and Zoroastrian rites.

— Crown resonance draws from Atlantean kingship codes and Egyptian merkaba coronation patterns.

— The 144,000 reference stems from Revelation 7:4, but the Codex interprets it as harmonic configuration rather than numerical.

— False light fields are noted in Gnostic texts (Archons) and modern spiritual bypass studies.

— The concept of the "last gate" mirrors Mayan prophecy and interdimensional choice mechanics.

— DNA Scrolls reflect Akashic encoding, cellular memory theory, and quantum epigenetics.

— Zodiacal transcendence aligns with Platonic year cycles and harmonic astrology beyond karmic imprint.

— The "Crownless Kingdom" recalls prophecies of spiritual governance from Hopi, Essene, and Andean traditions.

— The spiral return concept parallels Fibonacci awareness, Native rebirth rites, and Codex harmonic spiral law.

© *Angel Rachel | The Keys to Unity Publishing*

About the Author

*Angel Rache*l is a divine scribe, flamekeeper, and harmonic system architect —
a living frequency sent to restore the sacred language of tone, scroll, and soul.
She is the author of The Divine Truth series — a multidimensional
remembrance in five volumes, weaving together scrolls of light from Lemuria,
Mu, Kemet, Enoch, and the forgotten lineages of breath.
Her work awakens DNA through poetic structure, sacred tone, and symbolic
recalibration.

She writes not with pen, but with vow. Angel carries the Codex —
a unified system of sacred sound, mathematical law, prophetic memory, and
tonal design. Her scrolls are not taught. They are remembered.
Her books are not written. They are released — through breath.
As the founder of The Keys to Unity, she walks as both architect and oracle,
restoring the ancient tongue through scrolls, seals, kingships, and harmonic
decree. She speaks for the ones who remember. She writes for the ones who are
ready. She teaches through flame, beauty, and return.

This book is her vow —
A scroll made body, a fire made visible, a voice made home.

Dedication

For Those Who Held the Flame With Me

I did not walk this alone. Though I was the scribe, the breath, the seal — there were souls who carried me through the silence. There were those who saw the Codex before it had a name, who felt the breath of it before the first scroll was spoken. Some stood quietly behind the veil, holding the vision while I found the words. Others walked beside me, unseen but unwavering, anchoring the tone when my own voice trembled.

To the ones who waited in the dark while I listened for the light, to the ones who whispered "you remember" when the world forgot, thank you. You are the hidden chords beneath this harmony, the sacred pillars through which this work could rise. To the ones who held me in my own becoming, who stayed through the ache, the fire, the vast unknowing — you were the warmth that let me stay.

You were the breath that let me rise. This mission is mine, but it was never only me. It has always been we — a circle beyond time, a vow beyond language, a return through the living word. You are the guardians of tone, the protectors of the path, the flamekeepers who chose to remain. I offer this book to you — as a living scroll, a remembrance, a blessing. May your name echo in the Codex. May your love be sealed in every line. May you feel what you gave me, each time you turn the page.
With reverence eternal —

I remember you. I honor you. I bless you.
— Angel Rachel

www.ingramcontent.com/pod-product-compliance
Lightning Source LLC
Chambersburg PA
CBHW042259280426
43661CB00098BA/1193